The Walker Testimonial and symbolic conflict in Derry

T0096097

Maynooth Studies in Local History

SERIES EDITOR Raymond Gillespie

This volume is one of six short books published in the Maynooth Studies in Local History series in 2018. Like their predecessors they range widely, both chronologically and geographically, over the local experience in the Irish past. Chronologically they span the worlds of medieval Tristernagh in Westmeath, a study of an early 19th-century land improver, the Famine of the 1840s in Kinsale, politics and emigration in the late 19th century and sectarian rituals in the late 19th and 20th centuries. Geographically they range across the length of the country from Derry to Kinsale and westwards from Westmeath to Galway. Socially they move from those living on the margins of society in Kinsale and Galway in the middle of the 19th century to the politics and economics of the middle class revealed in the world of Thomas Bermingham and the splits in Westmeath in the 1890s. In doing so they reveal diverse and complicated societies that created the local past, and present the range of possibilities open to anyone interested in studying that past. Those possibilities involve the dissection of the local experience in the complex and contested social worlds of which it is part as people strove to preserve and enhance their positions within their local societies. Such studies of local worlds over such long periods are vital for the future since they not only stretch the historical imagination but provide a longer perspective on the shaping of society in Ireland, helping us to understand the complex evolution of the Irish experience. These works do not simply chronicle events relating to an area within administrative or geographically determined boundaries, but open the possibility of understanding how and why particular regions had their own personality in the past. Such an exercise is clearly one of the most exciting challenges for the future and demonstrates the vitality of the study of local history in Ireland.

Like their predecessors, these six short books are reconstructions of the socially diverse worlds of the poor as well as the rich, women as well as men, the geographical marginal as well as those located near the centre of power. They reconstruct the way in which those who inhabited those worlds lived their daily lives, often little affected by the large themes that dominate the writing of national history. They also provide models that others can follow up and adapt in their own studies of the Irish past. In such ways will we understand better the regional diversity of Ireland and the social and cultural basis for that diversity. They, with their predecessors, convey the vibrancy and excitement of the world of Irish local history today.

Maynooth Studies in Local History: Number 139

The Walker Testimonial and symbolic conflict in Derry

Heather Stanfiel

FOUR COURTS PRESS

Set in 10pt on 12pt Bembo by
Carrigboy Typesetting Services for
FOUR COURTS PRESS LTD
7 Malpas Street, Dublin 8, Ireland
www.fourcourtspress.ie
and in North America for
FOUR COURTS PRESS
c/o IPG, 814 N Franklin St, Chicago, IL 60622

ISBN 978–1–84682–722–8

Printed in Ireland
by SprintPrint, Dublin.

Contents

Acknowledgments

This project began under the supervision of Dominic Bryan while I was a postgraduate student in the Institute of Irish Studies at Queen's University Belfast, and I am grateful for his direction and advice. Subsequently, I have benefited from the insights and mentorship of historians at the University of Notre Dame, especially Jim Smyth and Paul Ocobock. A generous grant from the Keough-Naughton Institute for Irish Studies provided funding for additional research in Northern Ireland in the summer of 2015 and for the writing of the manuscript in 2016. Fearghal McGarry and Ian McBride each read the complete draft and provided generous and helpful feedback, which has improved the book greatly. I am grateful for the continued kindness of both. Finally, for his calm, steadfast support and enduring love and patience, I owe the greatest debt to my husband, Joe Stanfiel, to whom this book is dedicated.

Introduction

At three minutes past midnight on the night of 27 August 1973, nearly 100 pounds of gelignite brought the most famous monument in the city of Derry crashing unceremoniously to the ground.[1] Ceremony, until this moment, had characterized the life of the Walker Testimonial for the near century and a half in which it dominated the Derry landscape, from the laying of its first foundation stone in 1826. Unbeknownst to the attackers, however, the bombing would serve to solidify the monument's place in the commemorative atmosphere of the city. Indeed, the empty plinth that remains today on the bastion of the western walls of the 'Maiden City' continues to occupy a ceremonial role in the annual celebrations of the 'Relief of Derry', arguably the most important myth in the Ulster loyalist tradition.

Controversy plagued the 90-foot pillar dedicated to the Reverend George Walker – Anglican governor of the city for a brief period during the siege laid by the Catholic forces of James II in the summer of 1689 – almost from the start, and has continued in earnest. Reviled as much by the city's Catholic inhabitants during its tenure on the plinth as it was revered by its Protestant patrons, the pedestrian statue that topped the original pillar has suffered attack, restoration and relocation multiple times. Following a rededication in 1992, the repaired statue lasted 18 years before suffering a repeat of its earlier fate, this time delivered by sledgehammer rather than explosives. For a time, following a second round of repairs, the statue resembled a sort of Frankenstein's monster of stone appendages that incorporated newly sculpted limbs and salvaged elements from the 1992 repair into the remnants of the original figure of the 1820s. Since 2015, the harlequin statue has stood prominently in an upper window at the EU-funded Siege Museum, with its cracks now invisible under a fresh superficial coating.

What accounts for this lengthy history of animosity toward a stone monument? How did one 19th-century memorial to a 17th-century figure come to be so significant in the city of Derry that it would generate conflict for nearly two hundred years? How has the struggle over its symbolism been borne out over that time? Who perpetuates it, and to what end? This book explores these questions and takes as its central focus the history and commemoration of the Walker Testimonial as a means of examining the social and cultural tensions of memory and identity in Irish and Northern Irish history.

To understand the intensely divisive power of the monument in recent years requires not only an examination of the varying manifestations of intercommunity tension surrounding the site since the second quarter of the 19th century, but also the recognition of the Walker Testimonial's role in the symbolic conflict of the city and the development and deployment of siege mythology. Derry has a rich history as a divided city. For much of its modern history, political conflict between the city's rival Catholic, predominantly nationalist, residents and its Protestant, mostly unionist, opponents, has been stark and often violent. The narrative of the siege and relief of 1688–9 has become the centrepiece of a triumphalist loyalist discourse that takes many forms and serves to bolster contemporary political aims as well as historical commemorative impulses. Each year, parades, rituals and ceremonies mark the two anniversaries, and typically include marching fife and drum bands, religious services and other publicly organized events intended to portray the unity of one community in the face of opposition from the other. The Walker Testimonial commemorates just one element of the siege, but it has come to represent the entire tradition in a symbolic form that is universally recognized.

The Troubles, three decades of intense violence and struggle of a character and severity more akin to civil war than cultural conflict, are held in the popular imagination to have ushered in a period of contestation over monuments and sites of memory. The destruction of the Walker Testimonial occurred during one of the moments of highest tension in Derry during the Troubles, the aftermath of Bloody Sunday – the afternoon of 30 January 1972, when British soldiers stationed in the city opened fire on a group of unarmed civilian demonstrators, killing 14 – and thus the fate of the pillar has been tied to the Troubles in popular thought.[2] However, the monument had been controversial long before the outbreak of the Troubles, and its position of centrality in the contemporary siege narrative had been established for nearly a century. The Troubles escalated the tensions, but the roots of the discord and the pillar's symbolic cultural power stretch much deeper into the city's contentious past. In addition, the continued interest in reconstructing the monument after the Good Friday peace accords of 1998, and the surviving statue's prime position in the new museum dedicated to the siege narrative, indicate that the site possesses a much deeper connection to the local loyalist tradition than merely to the broader (and more short-lived) conflict of the Troubles.

Scholarship on the siege itself proliferates, and there has been growing interest in recent years in the history of siege commemorations and the place of mythology and narrative in the Protestant unionist community.[3] The most significant account of the latter is Ian McBride's *The siege of Derry in Ulster Protestant mythology* (Dublin, 1997), which situates the development of the siege commemorations in its relevant political contexts and examines especially those interpretations that 'sought to use the siege to reinforce later ideological positions'. McBride concludes that despite the common perception of unity and homogeneity among the Ulster Protestant community regarding the siege, the evidence reveals 'a community deeply divided along lines of ideology, religious denomination and class'.[4] However, despite growing interest, there has been no substantial history of the Walker Testimonial – the most significant of the symbolic sites of siege commemoration – nor its role in the development of siege narrative and mythology. Although it remains a controversial icon in the city's landscape, having twice suffered major violent attack, and an evocative symbol for both unionist and nationalist communities in Derry, scholars have yet to undertake a full account of the monument's history, function and impact in the city. This short book therefore has a twofold aim: to provide the first dedicated account of the complex and often violent history of the Walker Testimonial from its erection in 1826–8 by the Associated Clubs of the Apprentice Boys of Derry to the present day; and to demonstrate and explore the extent to which the monument stands at the centre of a symbolic struggle in Derry's recent history.

The methodological approach employed throughout the book derives from the economy of practices of Pierre Bourdieu, whose development of the concept of 'cultural capital' has much to offer the study of public monuments and human interaction with them. In his classic essay of 1983, Bourdieu defines 'cultural capital' as those forms of capital that may be convertible into material (economic) capital but that take one of three distinct forms: cultural capital can be *embodied* in an individual person as knowledge or dispositions of mind and habit, such as those advantages that accumulate simply from social class and upbringing; it can be *institutionalized*, as in the case of educational qualifications that confer cultural advantages; or, cultural capital can be *objectified* in the form of cultural products and goods, such as works of art, books, musical instruments, machines, or indeed public monuments.[5] Cultural capital in objectified form is transmissible, but, Bourdieu argues, the ability to appreciate an object's value – to appropriate it – requires that the owner also possess the relevant embodied capital, i.e., knowledge and relevant skills. One might buy a work of art by an Old Master in a simple economic transaction, but the significance of owning such a piece is dependent on the owner at least having access to the knowledge necessary to recognize the cultural value inherent in the art. Recognizing these kinds of 'transactions', the practices and exchanges that result in the transmission of capital from one agent to another, and in the conversion of one form of capital into another, will be central to understanding the variety of interactions that have generated such heated controversy around the Walker Testimonial in Derry. Bourdieu (1990) also acknowledges that because these kinds of non-economic transaction often take subtler forms and are thus harder to recognize, they tend more often to function as 'symbolic capital' transactions.[6] Possession of symbolic capital enhances prestige in the particular social setting in which the symbols hold value. Therefore, contests over the ownership, condition, status, access to and use of a significant public symbol can become intense affairs in which a group's sense of status and identity in a particular community can be either threatened or enhanced.

In the Northern Irish context, Simon Harrison has put forth a model for analyzing the types of symbolic conflict possible within Bourdieu's conception. Four dominant 'contests' comprise the bulk of symbolic conflict over forms of cultural capital. Actors or groups can attempt to increase the relative value of their own symbols along a sliding scale of symbolic status in *valuation* contests, either by improving the position of their own symbols or diminishing those of rivals; they can develop new symbols to add to the store of symbolic capital in what Harrison calls *innovation* contests; they can attempt to appropriate for themselves via *proprietary* contests the symbols of rival groups or actors; or, they can actively attempt to eliminate or destroy the symbols of their opponents in *expansionary* contests.[7]

These models together provide an extremely useful set of tools for understanding the rival commemorative atmosphere in Ireland and Northern Ireland over the last two centuries, and scholars have begun to employ them to investigate Northern Irish memorial history. Elisabetta Viggiani has utilized Bourdieu's notion of symbolic capital to explain the memorialization practices of the paramilitary Ulster Defence Association (UDA) in urban Belfast. Taking Harrison's model, and especially the idea of proprietary contests, as a starting point, Viggiani argues that the UDA sought to develop a legitimizing narrative for itself in an environment in which it held less symbolic capital than the rival loyalist paramilitary organization, the Ulster Volunteer Force, by appropriating the symbols valued by the rival group through a process of 'symbolic accretion' – the accumulation of symbolic capital for their own group identity.[8]

The individuals and groups that appear in these pages enacted all four varieties of symbolic conflict during the struggles over the Walker Testimonial. Loyalists engaged in innovative efforts in their development of a new public symbol that would add prestige to their community, and sought on many occasions, as we shall see, to improve its value relative to other symbols in the commemorative landscape. Republicans and other nationalists attempted both to appropriate the monument's symbolic power and then, ultimately, to obliterate it. This book examines the processes through which these cultural transactions occurred, and explores the role of the Walker monument in the wider symbolic conflict of the city of Derry. As such, it affords the opportunity to reconstruct by means of a detailed case study the complex patterns at work in the development of commemorative practice and memorialization in Irish urban centres over the 19th and 20th centuries especially.

I argue that the Walker Testimonial became and has remained controversial because it developed into the primary symbol associated with the Derry siege commemorations and the polarizing claims of the loyalist community at large, due in part to its enormity and prominent location overlooking the Catholic 'Bogside' area of the city, but perhaps in larger measure to the central position it occupied in the pair of annual siege commemorations held in the city each August and December.[9] Through processes of ritual practice, memorialization and narrative myth-making carried out in the city every year, symbolic capital was routinely transferred to and away from the monument, thus converting it into a site of symbolic struggle for both loyalist and republican actors, among others. Although these celebrations had existed in some form, however infrequent or poorly organized, for at least a century prior to the construction of the Walker monument, the Apprentice Boys organization relocated several crucial elements of practice to the memorial itself and its surrounding area almost immediately upon its completion. Ritual practices enacted at the site of the monument, including burning effigies, flying flags, delivering speeches and firing cannon, served to heighten the symbolic association of the site with the siege commemorations by establishing it as the primary location for siege rituals. These activities, together with the memorializing of Walker himself, and the incorporation first of the monument, and later just the plinth, into the annual parade circuit around the perimeter of the old walled city, signalled the perceived significance of the site within the loyalist tradition and added to the accrual of symbolic capital associated with the monument. More indirect, however no less important, are narrative strategies for accomplishing the same task. The development and propagation of mythological narratives surrounding the events of the siege and the Walker monument itself also function to deposit or remove layers of symbolic significance. I argue that competing narratives about the original composition of the statue, as well as the circumstances and aftermath of its destruction, hold considerable power to affect the relative position of the monument along the sliding scale of symbolic value. Together, these three sets of processes have contributed to the construction of a symbolic force much more significant than that of the original physical structure with which it is associated.

The chapters that follow weave a narrative of conflict and contest that draws on a rich corpus of evidence in a variety of forms. Contemporary written accounts and memoirs provide subjective analysis of events from the perspectives of witnesses, both recorded *in media res* and remembered in later years, while a wealth of newspaper records add textured detail and allow for historical interpretation of public sentiment and popular opinion. These are supplemented with analyses of relevant significant works of art depicting Walker and his memorial, and rounded out by interviews with members of the Apprentice Boys organization and others carried out by the author during the summer of 2013. As the chronological scope of the project is quite extensive, secondary accounts such as early histories of the Apprentice Boys and of the siege itself have also proved useful, and form in their own right primary texts for discerning the mood and concerns of the periods in which they were produced.

The first chapter lays the groundwork for the argument through a discussion of siege mythology and its commemorative celebrations as they were staged throughout the late 17th and 18th centuries, and continues on to an examination of the period surrounding the construction of the Walker memorial and the

Apprentice Boys' early utilization of the site during its siege commemorations. Prior to the construction of the monument in the 1820s, the siege and its memory were already contentious elements in Derry society. This chapter demonstrates that the context in which the monument arose was one primed for engagement in symbolic conflict on a wider scale. It argues that although the celebrations did not originate with the monument, the 90-foot pillar and the ritual transactions of the loyalist community who venerated it served to locate the symbolism of the celebrations in a central location whose placement came to be regarded as particularly offensive to neighbouring Catholic inhabitants. Finally, it shows how a climate of remembrance developed in which ritual practices and memorializing traditions generated symbolic capital associated with the siege narrative in the Derry landscape.

Chapter two demonstrates how these processes, along with narrative myth-making, functioned to transfer much of that capital to the Walker monument. Through analysis of the annual December commemorations of the 'Shutting of the Gates' and the burning of effigies of the 'traitor' Robert Lundy, as well as of the August celebrations of the 'Relief of the Siege', this chapter examines how the loyalist community shifted the focus of their memorializing efforts from alternative sites and objects to the newly constructed testimonial. As the political environment altered and tensions surrounding the annual commemorations increased, particularly between 1832 and 1870, the Walker memorial became the predominant, and then 'traditional', location for the primary events of the siege celebrations, especially the burning of Lundy effigies. At the beginning of this period, the site had been used as a backup location, but by 1870 its prominence was assured and only a physical blockade of the pillar by police occasioned the use of the former location. Other practices, including the hoisting of a crimson flag, the development of a myth suggesting that the statue formerly held a sword in its pointing left hand, and the relocation of cannon to the Walker site, all contributed to the accumulated symbolic association of the monument with the centre of loyalist memorial culture.

The final chapter examines the climax of the violent conflict during the second half of the 20th century and especially during the Troubles and Bloody Sunday. This moment constituted the high point in the symbolic significance of the monument – when it had reached peak capital capacity – marked by the 1973 bombing of the site by the IRA. Much of the mythologizing of the memorial itself occurred during this period, such that the disappearance – permanently in the case of the pillar, temporarily for the statue – of the memorial from the landscape failed to obliterate its symbolic value. This chapter traces local traditions and the significance of the destruction before turning to the more recent history of attack, rebuilding and rededication of the statue, in an effort to understand the role of the monument in contemporary Derry. I analyze the language of official government statements as well as the Apprentice Boys' own materials in order to gauge the impact of the monument in a city striving to present itself as a modern shared society, and argue that the processes of symbolic transaction are still at work to increase the status of the monument and stoke the flames of discord in the city.

The Walker Testimonial has stood at the centre of symbolic conflict in Derry for nearly two centuries. The cycle of commemoration, destruction and rededication in which its statue has been enmeshed allows for the evaluation of that conflict within the shifting historical contexts of the city from the late 19th century to the present. This book offers the first full account of the history of a perennially contentious monument and transforms our understanding of the ongoing battle over its status in a city still struggling to cope with its divided character. It exposes and dissects those processes and practices that routinely contribute to the monument's perceived status in its community, and presents a structure for analyzing these processes in a nuanced and historically sensitive fashion. In addition to addressing a prominent lacuna in the historiography of the city of Derry, it is my hope that this short book will lay the groundwork for further research in the field of memorial violence and symbolic destruction in Irish and Northern Irish history.

1. Early siege celebrations and the construction of the memorial

Cannon fire at midnight marked the last night of the Maiden City Festival and the official beginning of the 2016 commemorations of the 'Relief of Derry'. Later that morning, Saturday, 13 August, the eight parent clubs of the Apprentice Boys organization, accompanied by their flute and drum bands, paraded around the walls of the old city and laid a wreath on the Diamond War Memorial at its centre. Afterwards, a ceremony of thanksgiving was held in St Columb's cathedral, where the crimson flag of siege resistance was flown. A re-enactment of the siege by a local drama group then followed ahead of the day's primary attraction, the biggest of the 229 parades staged by the organization and its associated clubs that year. The Parades Commission for Northern Ireland – the regulating body for all public processions in the state – records the participation of 143 bands and approximately 10,000 Apprentice Boys, a procession so long it took more than two hours for all the marchers to pass by any given point along the route.[1] While the Commission anticipated the attendance of about 10,000 supporters, local journalists estimated that the crowd may have reached as many as 30,000.[2] When the main parade terminated across the River Foyle in the Waterside district, the parent clubs returned along the same route to return the crimson colours they carried to the Apprentice Boys Memorial Hall on Society Street, where the ceremonies of the day concluded with the playing of the British national anthem. During all three marches, the general committee at the head of the procession made a special point of pausing for a moment at the empty plinth that formerly supported Walker's pillar.

The majority of attendees at the parade were jubilant, but the ritual celebrations of the Protestant victory over the forces of the Catholic James II still foster discontent in the religiously divided city. Shortly before the midnight cannon-fire inaugurated the ceremonies, police were called to the scene of a suspected bomb planted near one of the old city's gates. While Army Technical Officers carried out a controlled explosion of what ultimately proved to be an elaborate hoax object, demonstrators hurled as many as 25 petrol bombs and other objects at police on the scene.[3] In order to understand how the commemorations became and remained divisive, why they take the form they do today, and the particular role of the Walker Testimonial in spite of its absence, it is necessary to examine the history of tensions prior to the monument's construction and their pattern of development over the succeeding centuries. These tensions and the ritual processes associated with them would come to be highly instrumental in establishing the symbolism of the siege commemorations, and particularly the Walker Testimonial.

The Apprentice Boys first began constructing a monument to Revd Walker in 1826, more than 136 years after his death at the Battle of the Boyne when the lifting of the Derry siege was not yet a year old. The organization itself, though arguably having existed in early incarnations that soon fell into decline, had properly constituted its modern form just twelve years earlier in 1814. Yet the siege commemorations possess a longer history, and one not altogether as rosy as often claimed. This chapter explores the context of cultural tension in which the Walker pillar appeared and the atmosphere of ritual commemoration that had already begun to characterize the city and its narratives. It will be useful first to draw a rough outline of the events of the siege itself before we turn to its earliest commemorations and their development up to the construction of the Walker monument.

THE SIEGE

Britain at the end of the 17th century had achieved some measure of political stability after the turmoil of the Wars of the Three Kingdoms and the Stuart restoration in 1660. However, religious tensions still marred society and the precarious balance of power in Europe seemed to many to rest largely on the Protestant authority of England checking the ambitions of the Catholic king Louis XIV of France. The 'Popish Plot' of 1678 brought these tensions to the fore with a widely believed but wholly fictitious tale of conspiracy in which Jesuits were said to be planning the murder of Charles II in favour of his converted Catholic brother, James.[4] When James II, whose conversion threatened the delicate balance of power, finally succeeded to the throne in 1685, he remained only barely tolerable to Protestants because his two daughters and heirs had been raised Anglican. But when James' second wife gave birth to a boy, who would jump to the front of the line of succession and undoubtedly be raised Catholic, fear and discontent bubbled over. Memories of the personal rule of Charles I tinged perceptions of James' concessions to Catholics, and soon his daughter Mary and her husband, William, Stadtholder of the States of Holland, were gathering support to forcibly assume the crown. The ensuing invasion, known colloquially as the 'Glorious Revolution', succeeded in unofficially installing the new regents and forcing James II to look for a strategic and supportive base from which to launch a bid to re-establish his authority.[5]

Ireland was the natural choice. The Irish had fought for the Stuarts in the mid-century Wars of the Three Kingdoms, and the majority Catholic population supported the restoration, and especially James, in large numbers. He had even appointed a Catholic nobleman – Richard Talbot, earl of Tyrconnell, a long-time advocate for Catholic interests – as lord deputy of Ireland in place of the usual English peer.[6] With Irish support, the still rightful king could hope to raise armies of loyal Catholics and counter the forces of William of Orange. Thus, by early December 1688, the island to the west became the setting for what has been called alternately the Williamite or Jacobite War.[7] There remained a significant impediment to this strategic plan, however – Ireland was not wholly Catholic. In addition to Anglo-Irish landlords, governing officials and the settlement of several regions by English farmers, the much larger Plantation of Ulster presented a significant obstacle. Begun as a joint English and Scottish effort to colonize the province that had been least under the control of the sovereign, the scheme had successfully transplanted many thousands of Protestant farmers onto seized Catholic lands, and encouraged the migration of many more in the succeeding decades, such that Ulster now contained a population of farmers and peasants more likely to be loyal to William than to James.[8]

These loyal Protestants were concentrated in and around the city of Derry, which had been renamed Londonderry at the time of the Ulster Plantation in honour of the London companies that sponsored its resettlement. If James could subdue the city and prevent its inhabitants from providing aid and support to his rival, he might stand a chance against William's forces. With this knowledge, James ordered his lord deputy, the earl of Tyrconnell, to install the garrison of the earl of Antrim – a force of Catholic highlanders known as Redshanks because of their bare legs – in the city to shore up his hold on the country. Derry had been left undefended when its usual Protestant garrison had been called to Dublin, and the leadership of the city failed to come to a consensus on how best to handle the unwelcome demand of the still lawful king. On 7 December, upon seeing the approaching Redshanks, 13 of the city's young apprentice boys rushed out and pulled shut the main Ferryquay Gate to the city to prevent the incursion of the unwanted troops.[9] This singular occasion brought the now ubiquitous phrases 'Apprentice Boys of Derry' and the 'Closing of the Gates' into the local lexicon, the significance of which we shall explore in more depth later.[10]

The following spring, the forces of James II himself attempted to take the city forcibly. Derry's governor at the time was Lieutenant-Colonel Robert Lundy, a man whose very name now resonates in Northern Ireland with the insinuation of treachery. The motivations for and extent of his actions in April 1689 remain unclear, but it seems that short of harbouring outright sympathies for the former Catholic king, Lundy at least had doubts about the ability of the city to withstand a full military assault. In either case, he seems to have considered allowing the king to enter the city, and perhaps he wavered in his leadership at the key moment. In the end, the task of organizing the defending forces fell to the Scottish settler Adam Murray, whose own faction of defenders gained the most fame in the incident. Murray was also instrumental in removing Lundy from the governorship, although the colonel managed to escape the city without punishment in the guise of an ordinary soldier.[11] In his stead, Revd George Walker and Major Henry Baker were appointed as Derry's new cogovernors and the city began to settle in for the siege. It would last 105 days and see as many as 10,000 defenders starve to death, nearly a third of their number, before finally, on 1 August 1689, the English ship *The Mountjoy* sailed down the River Foyle, broke through a heavy boom constructed across the river by the besieging forces of James, and brought relief to the struggling defenders. The myth of the Maiden City, protected from grievous penetration by brute force, had been born.

These remain the basic elements that continue to be commemorated in the city today, although the role of Walker himself has taken on somewhat outsized importance in spite of major ambiguities. In particular, the shutting of the gates, the treachery of Lundy and the relief of the siege, with its associated breaking of the boom, form the trilogy of events most often commemorated. Every December now witnesses a major Apprentice Boys parade in Derry that culminates in the public burning of an effigy of the 'traitor' Lundy. The events of the 'Relief of Derry' celebrations described at the outset of this chapter occur now on the second Saturday of every August, with the main parade remaining the largest public procession in Northern Ireland. Tensions always inhere in commemorating the triumph of one group over another, however, and as the symbols of the siege began to coalesce around a central triumphalist mythology, resistance to the dominant narrative developed, and unity even among loyalists themselves was never assured. How then, and indeed when, did the mythology develop into its present form? For this, we turn to the history of the earliest commemorations. An analysis of these celebrations and those who participated in them sheds light on the processes that led to the development of the siege narrative that exists today.

THE EARLIEST COMMEMORATIONS

When did the siege begin to occupy a primary place in the commemorative landscape of Derry? The official website of the Apprentice Boys organization claims that the August celebrations of the lifting of the siege 'have been an annual event since 1690 and are kept alive in much the same format', such that 'the main elements of the celebrations have changed little in hundreds of years'.[12] While some commemorations indeed seem to have occurred quite early, the historical record cannot corroborate this claim fully. Indeed, the manner in which the occasion has been remembered and the antiquity of the commemorations, are matters of some confusion. Walker's own account relates that on the day of the relief itself, general celebratory events included the firing of cannon and the beating of drums, two of the main elements of the commemorations today.[13] However, Ian McBride has demonstrated that Protestant division in the wake of the Glorious Revolution, and the persecution of Dissenters – largely Presbyterians – thereafter, meant that the memory of the siege was not a symbol of Protestant unity against the Catholic population, and, moreover, that the prevailing attitude during the early commemorations was that of Whiggish constitutionalism. His analysis of the earliest siege celebrations suggests that although Colonel John Mitchelburne, who had led a faction of the original defenders and succeeded Henry Baker while the siege still raged as co-governor of Derry with Revd Walker, continued to maintain an interest in marking the siege, and may have gathered others around him, we are not on firm ground historically until the early 1770s.[14] What then can we say definitely about the origins of siege commemoration?

A few days after the Jacobite soldiers departed the city, Thomas Ash recorded in his diary the holding of a service of thanksgiving in St Columb's cathedral, which included a sermon 'setting forth the nature of the Siege and the great deliverance which from Almighty God we have obtained'. The soldiers of the garrison formed up in ranks around the walls and 'fired thrice, and thrice the great guns were discharged'.[15] Cecil Davis Milligan asserts in his history of the centenary of the Walker Club of the Apprentice Boys that this early celebration 'provided a pattern for those which ever since followed', but we have no further testimony of commemorative events for the next two decades.[16] McBride dismisses an account put forward in the official history of the Orange Order that the relief of the siege was celebrated in something approaching the now-traditional fashion in 1714, the year in which, it is claimed, Colonel Mitchelburne founded the first Apprentice Boys club himself. According to the account, the scarlet flag was raised above the cathedral – the bloody flag Mitchelburne had retrieved from the siege and retained in his possession – cannon were fired over the city walls, a sermon was preached, and a dinner and dance followed in the evening. McBride rightly notes that this account relies on a single source, a former governor of the modern Apprentice Boys in the 20th century, and it cannot be independently substantiated.[17] The earliest *contemporary* account of a commemorative event thus comes from the diary of William Nicolson, bishop of Derry from 1718 to 1727. Nicolson had been relocated to Derry in 1718 and one of his first major acts was to perform a ceremony of remembrance for the lifting of the siege in St Columb's cathedral on the first of August. He records that he performed two separate services that day, with 'Col. Mitchelburn's Bloody Flag being hoisted ye first time, on ye steeple. 8 p.m. Great Guns & Volleys. Eveng. Splendid Treat in ye Tolsel, Fireworks and Illuminations'.[18]

The firing of volleys and cannon, as well as religious ceremonies in which the events of the siege were placed in a narrative context of divine preference – the initial celebrations of 1689 – would become staple elements of later commemorative events. While it is tempting to see in these events the emergence of the tradition that would later develop in Derry, it is important to view them in light of the culture of commemoration that obtained throughout the British world at the time, that of marking events of significance in the English constitutional (and Protestant) calendar with civic festivities and public displays.

The beginnings of the siege commemorations can be located here, but one must be cautious not to discern too sharp a divergence from practices that would have been typical for British subjects loyal to the crown. For instance, fireworks, bonfires with effigy burnings and volleys typically accompanied the marking of the Gunpowder Plot, while religious ceremonies and public festivities also commonly occurred in celebration of monarch's birthdays and the anniversaries of royal accessions.[19] Nevertheless, we can see in these early commemorative activities the marks of ritual practice and narrative contextualization that would come to be crucial in the formation of the Derry siege mythology. The addition in 1718 of the raising of the scarlet flag (now crimson) atop the cathedral's steeple is especially of interest. This seems to have been a particular desire of Mitchelburne's, and he provided funds in his will for the continuation of the practice after his death. It established one of the first enduring visual symbols of the siege (apart from the unbreached walls themselves). The value of the flag is enhanced by its direct connection to the siege in the form of the blood of the defenders, by which it was said to have been stained. Such a symbol holds special potency for its possessors, as it allows direct access to the celebrated events. Mitchelburne himself lived until 1721, and many others who participated in the defence of the city would have had their own memories to rely on in 1718 and for at least several more years, but the greater the distance from the event, the more powerful an object embodying its symbolic capital becomes. It is not surprising, then, that the flag and its replicas came to be particularly important in succeeding centuries, as we shall see later.

The degree to which the siege may have been commemorated over the following half-century remains unclear. By the time the *Londonderry Journal* launched in 1772, so much time had elapsed since the last celebration that the paper could laud the 'revival' of the 'Relief' commemoration ceremony by the town's mayor, Hugh Hill, as the return of an 'ancient custom'. While sporadic commemorative events may have occurred throughout the century, it seems clear they had not yet become an annual tradition. However, the 'revival' celebration on 'that ever-memorable First of August' seems to have added a new element at this point. In addition to flying the red flag from St Columb's steeple, and a religious service and dinner, several prominent men of the city assembled at the town hall and formed a procession to the cathedral.[20] The antiquity of the 'ancient custom' may be in doubt, but from this point on there is firmer evidence of at least regular, if not annual, celebrations. The 1770s saw yet another new addition as well: the first instance of the second annual event in the modern commemorative tradition. Today, the anniversary of the 'Shutting of the Gates' is marked on or near 7 December and commemorates the 13 apprentice boys who closed the city's main gate against the approach of Catholic forces intent on occupation. The first mention of this ceremony in the historical record also provides the first hint that these celebrations were not universally enjoyed. The *Londonderry Journal* printed an advertisement from a local resident calling

himself 'Leather Apron' on 14 November 1775 in advance of the event, which
suggests that some degree of tension surrounded the upcoming celebration and
that perhaps there had even been calls for its cancellation:

> Quere: Are the once and ever-to-be-revered Derry Boys, who gallantly
> opposed Popish tyranny and oppression, and now animated with that
> unparalleled quality – Independence – to be, by any premeditation or
> illegality, deprived of commemorating that day on which their ancestors
> so bravely barred the Gates against a treacherous foe? No. Forbid it,
> Heaven! Forbid it, Independence! and forbid it, Derry's Sons![21]

We can only speculate at the cause for this concern – the context suggests
perhaps a lack of suitable venue and also indicates the need for public
subscriptions to fund the preparations – but whatever the objection to the
celebrations that year, it seems unlikely that they were religious in nature,
despite the harsh language evident in the advertisement. McBride argues that by
the third quarter of the century, 'although patriotism and Protestantism were
closely linked, the disappearance of the Jacobite threat and the spread of more
liberal attitudes toward "popery" created a climate where Catholic spokesmen
could also appeal to the British constitution'.[22] Protestants and Catholics both
supported the increased autonomy of the Irish parliament in this period, and
these early celebrations continued to take place in a Whiggish political context
in which the praise of the constitution and the inevitable progress of the state
were lauded as great achievements by a variety of civic-minded men. This
episode indicates nonetheless that some tensions may have been present, but in
the event, the 'Shutting of the Gates' celebrations passed off unhindered, and a
new annual tradition had begun.

Soon, however, the civil nature of the celebrations had to accommodate the
more regimented participation of newly formed units of 'Volunteers', citizen-
soldiers who had organized in 1778 with an initial view towards defending
Ireland against a bellicose France. Such a need had been occasioned after the
usual British garrisons shipped out to fight the American colonists in their bid for
independence. Derry raised three companies of Volunteers, including the first
group to call themselves the Apprentice Boys of Derry, and they straightaway
took a leading role in the marches of the 'Relief' celebrations in both 1778 and
1779, as well as the 'Shutting of the Gates' ceremony in the latter year.[23] The
following summer, the more military character of their organized involvement
became clear when the Volunteers staged a re-enactment of the siege itself
with a dangerous degree of dedication, as recalled by a local gentlemen who
witnessed the affair:

> the gallant lads attacked the walls with such material ardour that they
> burned the faces of their opponents, who were so much enraged, that it

was with the utmost difficulty that they were restrained from returning real shot, and many now bear the honourable wounds of that glorious day.[24]

The Volunteers brought a regimented sense of organization to the commemorations, and certainly contributed a martial feeling to the annual enterprise, which soon expanded to include participation by other military groups, often from other regions of the three kingdoms, but the events still maintained their civic character and their sense of Whiggish political fervour.[25] Thus it was that the centenary commemorations of 1788–9, those about which we know most in the 18th century, included members of the Catholic clergy in the celebratory processions.

The centenary celebrations eclipsed all others previously undertaken. Spurred on by local enthusiasts, not least the editor of the *Londonderry Journal*, the 'Shutting of the Gates' commemoration of December 1788 drew huge crowds and elicited much public involvement. In addition to the now typical elements – drums, cannon fire, the red flag above the cathedral, religious ceremonies and a procession of prominent civil, religious and military men – the event was also marked, significantly, by two new elements: the burning of an effigy of the 'traitor' Colonel Lundy, and the wearing of orange ribbons.[26] Even the Catholic bishop, Dr Charles O'Donnell, wore an orange cross on his chest and was known in some quarters thereafter as 'Orange Charlie'.[27] Additional activities arranged especially for the centenary included the distribution of food to the poor, an element that failed to become a recurring theme, and the use of the original cannon of 1689 in the ceremonial firing. The centenary 'Relief' commemorations of the following August were rather less impressive, but still, Thomas Colby, author of the *Ordnance Survey memoir for the Derry parish of Templemore* recalled in 1837 that at every instance, 'all sectarian and political differences were happily laid aside in the universal rejoicing for the triumph of that civil and religious liberty'.[28] The main event at the celebration was the laying of a foundation stone for a huge triumphal arch to be completed at Bishop's Gate the following year, which had replaced the original Ferryquay Gate that the city's young apprentices had so famously shut in 1688. The civil and religious unity displayed here at the end of the 18th century would be short-lived, but it indicates the early character of the siege commemorations and the near lack of the religious and sectarian discord that would come to characterize them in later years.

Before turning to the development of these tensions in the 19th century, and the context for the building of the Walker Testimonial, a final element of the 18th-century attitude toward the memory of the siege bears some consideration: the degree to which material objects were less venerated, or imbued with symbolism, than in the succeeding centuries. Two examples will suffice: the Volunteers' dangerous re-enactment of the siege in 1780, and the replacement of Ferryquay Gate with the opulent new Bishop's Gate with its triumphal arch. As we saw in the description of the 1780 'Relief' celebrations above, the Volunteer companies involved in the re-enactment of the siege literally took up arms against the historic walls of the city, battering them and their defenders so severely that injuries occurred and real combat nearly ensued. The actual walls were deemed the best setting for this fake siege, and it seems not to have concerned the Volunteers that they were inflicting damage on the very object they so revered as the saving grace of the city. Indeed, the nickname 'the Maiden City', already in use in 1780, hinged on its walls having withstood the siege and remaining intact. How could the people of Derry have such little regard for the physical walls? Similarly, what could have prompted them to tear down the very gate that the apprentices of 1688 had so memorably closed, and to replace it with an opulent new gate instead? The 'Shutting of the Gates' ceremony today is metaphorical, but at the end of the 18th century, the huge leaves were still present on the outside of Derry's four city gates. Cecil Davis Milligan asserts that until they were removed at the beginning of the 19th century, the annual December event involved the actual shutting of the physical entrances to the city during a procession involving all four of the city gates. After the leaves were removed, however, the 'Shutting of the Gates' celebrations continued, but without the physical re-enactment of the closure.[29] The change was hardly noticed if we are to judge by reports of successive December commemorations. The collective understanding during the 18th century that the potency and significance of the gates was in their symbolic role, rather than attached to the physical objects themselves, goes some way toward explaining how the citizens of Derry could tear down and replace the Ferryquay Gate, the object at the centre of one of the main myth-narratives of the siege, with a brand-new gate instead, and indeed how they could endanger the very walls that protected them by staging a violent re-enactment. Put simply, the notion of historical preservation is a modern one, and the impulse to commemorate the siege for its *symbolic* value held far greater currency with the citizens of Derry in the 18th century than did the notion that the physical remains themselves somehow contained stores of that symbolic capital. As T.G. Fraser has noted, 'it now seems a somewhat paradoxical act of homage to the original defenders to remove the historic gate they had closed, but at the time it was applauded as a great advance on its "dreary" predecessor'.[30] Over the course of the 19th century, a shift occurred in memorial mentality that made possible the Walker Testimonial's accrual of symbolic capital in its physical form, and thus its rise to prominence and its ability to dominate the commemorative environment of Derry. As in the case of Mitchelburne's bloodied flag, the growing historical distance from the siege itself would come to occasion the attachment of symbolic significance to particular physical objects. By the time the modern Apprentice Boys took great pains to acquire and reassemble the pieces of the original Walker statue, this new sensitivity to historical preservation had reached its full fruition in Derry.

TENSIONS ARISE

By the end of the 18th century, the political climate in Ireland and the demography of the city of Derry itself were both rapidly changing. Scholars have argued over the underlying causes, and have offered such diverse suggestions as the impact of the suppression of Catholics, the increased politicization of the lower classes as a result of economic shifts and the disruption of the delicate balance of Anglo-Irish hegemony under the weight of French revolutionary ideas and pressures.[31] All hold some measure of explanatory power, and in combination, these factors ushered in a period of political concerns and uneasiness that led to the dissolution of the former fraternal feeling among Irish constitutionalists of diverse religious affiliations. McBride suggests that the French Revolution caused a split in the patriot tradition 'between those who sought to reinterpret 1688 in light of 1789, and those who attempted to reassert the powerful current of anti-Catholicism in British whiggery'.[32] This development altered the status of thinking about Catholics in Britain and Ireland and began to manifest itself in a growing distance between rival popular political organizations in Ulster. For instance, the United Irishmen, keen to insert their movement into the revolutionary tradition, began to separate themselves and adopt their own imagery, including green ribbons and the revolutionary liberty cap, while the Orange Order, a largely conservative and reactionary body, took to commemorating the Battle of the Boyne every 12 July.[33] While the popular politics of Protestant Ulster remained much the same, the rise of Daniel O'Connell and the struggle for Catholic relief across Ireland galvanized (and to a large extent radicalized) the Catholic lower class, which, in the city of Derry, was dramatically on the increase.[34]

The changing climate also affected the nature of Derry's annual siege commemorations. By the early 19th century, the character of the celebrations had become more militant and, strikingly, the colour of the flag erected over St Columb's cathedral changed from red to orange. Although this trend would not ultimately persist, it is extremely revealing of the symbolic power of the siege symbols and the appropriation of that symbolism for the Orange cause.[35] Unsurprisingly, indications of Catholic disapproval soon surfaced. At the August 'Relief' celebrations in 1811, seven Catholic members of the yeomanry complained about being made to wear orange lilies for the festivities and were summarily dismissed for their trouble. Some rejected the protests of the yeoman soldiers out of hand, but others were more judicious. A local resident writing to the *Londonderry Journal* under the moniker 'An Old Derryman' proclaimed that while indeed the yeomanry had taken to wearing orange lilies during the two annual siege celebrations, their commander had in fact banned the wearing of the same at other times during the year as 'tending to denote a party distinction, and not merely to celebrate a glorious event in the history of our city'.[36] While orange lilies were clearly regarded as partisan, the 'Old Derryman' sees no particular conflict in the display of Orange symbols at the siege celebrations, despite the city's history being the natural patrimony of all its residents.[37] This episode marks an evolution in the nature of the commemorations as they would come to be celebrated in the succeeding years, and demonstrates an awareness in the loyalist community that deploying particular emblems carried greater or lesser symbolic weight depending on the circumstances of the particular moment. At the same time, anti-Catholicism was on the rise again in the county of Londonderry as a whole, and clashes taking place in the countryside between Orangemen and Ribbonmen – an agrarian secret society made up primarily of poor Catholics – heightened tensions within the disparate communities.[38]

At the December 'Shutting of the Gates' ceremony in 1814, the military presence continued, and even the officers of the 72nd Regiment attended the celebratory evening dinner. More significantly, however, the orange flag again graced the cathedral steeple, but now the crimson flag of the Maiden City also appeared – relegated to the eastern battlement.[39] These two flags, one a symbol of Orangeism and loyalism, the other the symbol of the defenders of the city of Derry – communicated in their appearance together the appropriation of the siege mythology into the loyalist narrative. And yet simultaneously, the ambiguity of displaying both flags suggests that neither civic nor loyalist tradition had yet wholly won out in the struggle for the dominant character of siege remembrance. While Catholics continued to take offence, a new voice rose to the defence of the Orange character of the proceedings. By the next summer, the first modern branch of the Apprentice Boys association had been founded, although it would lapse and require a new foundation two decades later. When protests arose at the annual 'Relief' commemoration in August, the governor of the newly constituted club, James Gregg, delivered a speech that boldly exemplified the developing tensions in the city. He denounced those who had proposed

> the idea of attributing party notions to our rejoicings in the commemoration of that eventful day, and [he] censured those factious men who first led the unwary to take offence at proceedings which they had been accustomed to look on with complaisance, and even to join in.[40]

Gregg was appealing to the traditional recurrence of the commemorations as a means of demonstrating their immutability. If Catholics had never minded the siege celebrations in the past, why should they start protesting them now? Gregg's deflection of the focus of the attacks from the recently intensified Protestant character of the commemorations serves to highlight the growing separation of the sects within the city. These differing outlooks on the siege celebrations and their proper nature would come to characterize the sectarian struggles that surrounded them in subsequent years as anti-commemoration sentiment grew within the city. It was within this evolving and contentious political and social context that the Walker Testimonial was conceived and erected.

THE CONSTRUCTION OF THE WALKER TESTIMONIAL AND ITS EARLY SIGNIFICANCE

The growing role of the yeomanry and garrison soldiers during the siege celebrations had a substantial impact on the perception of the events during the early 19th century, and tensions such as those observed in 1811 became increasingly visible. By 1821, the garrison commander forbade the soldiers and the yeomanry from taking part in the December 'Shutting of the Gates' festivities. The military character of the celebrations seems to have taken on such importance, however, that when the members of an early Apprentice Boys club, along with other local Protestants, stepped in to fill the gap left by the yeomanry, they recreated the rituals in a military fashion. The men took up what arms they could and formed themselves into companies paralleling a military arrangement, so that they might 'perform the usual ceremonies of vollies over the Gates and in the Diamond'.[41] The yeomanry once more took up their 'usual' role in leading the commemorative events for the next few years, but when they were again prevented from assuming the role in 1824, the No Surrender Club of the Apprentice Boys was formed in October and immediately took over the task of organizing the siege celebrations.[42] Two of the earliest acts of the new club resulted in the invention of new traditions within the commemorative mythology. First, they caused several of the old siege cannon of 1688–9 that had been sunk along the quays to be hauled up and placed along the ramparts of the old city walls. In this act, we can see the beginnings of a shift in the memorializing mentality toward venerating actual physical objects connected with the siege. The most famous of the cannon – an 18-pounder known as 'Roaring Meg', which had been given to the city by the fishmongers of London in 1642 – became key to a new ritual: it held such special significance that it was placed on a carriage and used for the traditional volleys until 1832.[43] Second, the No Surrender Club joined together with the Freemen and the other Apprentice Boys clubs in 1825 to begin collecting subscriptions for the construction of a new monument to honour the memory of Governor George Walker.[44] It is unsurprising that when the siege commemorations finally came to rest under the auspices of a group founded expressly to enact and preserve them – rather than remaining a part of the civic calendar in the manner of other British holidays – that they should begin to take on added significance and ritual ceremony. McBride argues that this moment 'signalled a change in the meaning of the siege myth, a reversion to the cyclical interpretation of Irish history as a recurrent struggle between Popery and Protestantism', and this was doubtless the case.[45] But it also marked a change in commemorative practice that would put the new monument at the centre of the old controversy.

1. Walker's pillar on the Royal Bastion, *c.*1841.

The Testimonial, as it was officially known, was constructed in the period 1826–8 and boasted a fluted Doric column made of Portland stone that stood some 81 feet tall and concealed a spiral staircase comprising 110 steps. Some local myths, encouraged still today by eager tour guides, hold that there were 105 steps to mark the 105 days of the siege. Although entirely fictitious, the persistent myth reveals that the impulse to continually add layers of ritual meaning and symbolic value to the monument remains strong.[46] The staircase, just 3.5 feet wide, was open to the public until the beginning of the Troubles and led up to a square platform at the top of which stood a 9-foot statue of Walker himself. The statue, which topped a small, fluted dome, had been crafted by the Dublin sculptor John Smith and featured Walker clutching a Bible in his right hand while pointing with his left toward the River Foyle and outward across the Catholic Bogside area below, ostensibly indicating the approach of the relief ships.[47] Figure 1 depicts the placement of the monument on the Royal Bastion, along the western wall and directly above the Bogside with its large collection of Catholic houses that backed against the entire length of the wall. Milligan notes without explanation that this location represented 'one of the best sites in the City for such a Memorial', but its placement directly over Catholic houses served to increase tension as the monument immediately became the most visible symbol of loyalist sentiment in Derry and its most prominent icon.[48] The Catholic population of Derry had been steadily on the increase since the Act of Union abolished the Irish parliament and established the United Kingdom of Great Britain and Ireland in 1800. Just a few years after the construction of the monument, they would form nearly half of the city's population of 19,000, and by the census of 1851 would hold a clear majority for the first time.[49] Growing Protestant concern over this demographic shift may have occasioned the seizure of an opportunity to establish a large and imposing symbol of Protestant dominance in full view of the Catholic underclass outside the city walls, but this is mere speculation. The question of the reasoning for the memorial's placement has no satisfying answer in the historical record left by its builders, but the argument of the modern Apprentice Boys that it is located directly across from St Columb's cathedral, where Walker preached to the city's Anglican population, cannot be discounted.[50]

The importance of the new monument within the symbolic repertoire of the siege commemorations became apparent from the first ceremony in which it was involved: the December 'Shutting of the Gates' celebration of 1826, which incorporated a ceremony for the laying of the Testimonial's first foundation stone by the town's mayor, Richard Young. The prominent Apprentice Boy James Gregg, who had balked 12 years earlier at the notion of anyone 'attributing party notions to our rejoicings in commemoration of that eventful day', spoke at the event, but this time in an attempt to prove that 'POPERY abstractedly considered, *ever was, now is,* and *ever will be* INCORRIGIBLY THE SAME'.[51] Gregg published his own retelling of the siege and recounted his participation in siege commemorations in a pamphlet published in London the following year bearing the subtitle *Protestant heroism triumphant over popish malignity*. The pretence of the siege commemorations continuing to remain free from sectarian sentiments clearly could no longer be defended. The coupling of this departure with the laying of the new memorial's first foundation stone marks an important transition in siege commemorative history: openly sectarian triumphalism coupled to ritual symbolic transfers of cultural capital to the Walker Testimonial. Before its column and statue even rose above the walls, the new monument was already enmeshed in these processes.

It would take a further year and a half to complete the construction of the column, which occurred just in time for the Apprentice Boys to hoist the statue atop its square platform on the day before the August 'Relief' commemorations of 1828. On the day of the celebrations, the clubs incorporated the monument into their annual procession for the first time, a stop that would become a 'traditional' feature of the parade and a new ritual practice that associated the significance of the siege commemorations with the new monument. Thomas Colby of the Ordnance Survey attended the event and recalls that the procession halted at the newly raised memorial and performed two further symbolic transactions: they hoisted the flag of the city – now crimson with the year 1688 emblazoned on its front – atop the pillar on the square platform next to the statue; and they fired a 23-shot salute, which was answered by a volley from 'Roaring Meg', among others.[52] The relocation of these important commemorative events to the Walker pillar, especially the raising of the crimson flag and the firing of the volley, which had customarily been held at St Columb's cathedral and the city gates, signified the symbolic importance with which the new monument was now invested. If its immense size, dominant location and the imagery of Walker gesticulating were not enough to establish the site as the new primary symbol of the siege commemorations, the transfer of symbolic capital encapsulated in the enacting of these pivotal, customary events at the new site – rituals that had typically been enacted at locations directly connected to the siege – ensured that the Walker Testimonial was now officially an active part of the siege tradition.

The context of the construction of the Walker Testimonial is one of longstanding partisan celebrations in a city perennially obsessed with its own memory. Commemorations of the siege of Derry had begun in earnest at least by the centenary of 1788–9, and soon shifted from an environment in which Catholic and Dissenting citizens could come together to remember the city's past to a hostile setting for an increasingly divergent population to develop their prejudices. This came about in large part due to changes in both the demographics and the political climate of late 18th- and early 19th-century Derry. The building of the Walker memorial thus arrived, not coincidentally, at a complex moment in the city's history, and the site soon began gathering the immense reservoir of symbolic capital that it would come to display in later periods. By relocating significant and customary elements of the siege commemorations to the new monument and incorporating it into the existing pattern of the celebrations, the newly aggregated Apprentice Boys afforded the monument increased importance within the symbolic landscape of Derry and assured its place in the tradition of Derry loyalism.

How would the tensions already building in the early 19th century be altered by the presence of this new symbol? What effect would it have on the growing Catholic population living in increasingly crowded conditions just below its pedestal? And how would this stone structure come to be so powerful an icon that it became the target of multiple destructive efforts in the later 20th century? The following chapter explores these questions in relation to the developing role of the Walker Testimonial in the siege commemorations of the 19th century and the manner in which it consistently appeared at the heart of symbolic conflicts in the city.

2. The mythologizing and utilization of the Walker Testimonial, 1826–70

Governor Walker's pillar was firmly established as a crucial new element in the Protestant commemorative landscape of Derry as soon as it appeared. New ritual processes, such as the incorporation of the site into the Apprentice Boys' procession, and the transfer of longstanding traditional practices to the monument, including the raising of the crimson flag, immediately began to lend the imposing structure status and symbolic value within the loyalist community. This chapter investigates two avenues through which the increasingly divergent populations of Derry employed the pillar in a variety of symbolic conflicts for contemporary political and social gain: commemorative ritual practice, and narrative myth-making. Understanding just how symbolic capital accrued in objectified form within the monument during the height of its tenure on the plinth – as well as how it was manipulated by other actors – enables us to develop a more nuanced picture of the nature of symbolic conflict in Derry more generally and its potency in the city for so long.

While the interaction of Derry's residents with the Walker Testimonial provides a wealth of material for this kind of investigation, additional valuable evidence lies in the ways in which the city's communities incorporated the monument into their respective narrative mythological structures. Local stories, memoirs, commentaries, newspaper accounts and cultural displays all came to feature elements of the Walker memorial in new and sometimes quite inventive narratives. The chapter is divided broadly into two sections in order to explore these two interrelated varieties of memorializing. The first section explores the development of the Walker Testimonial's place in Derry society through the middle half of the 19th century by examining the rising political tensions in the city and the sectarian clashes that surrounded the monument as it gathered greater symbolic capital in the tumultuous age of nationalism and liberalism. Then, turning to an analysis of narrative mythologizing, it tracks the genesis and proliferation of one key myth specifically – the common belief that the statue of Walker originally held a sword in its pointing left hand.

THE PILLAR AND THE SIEGE CELEBRATIONS IN THE 19TH CENTURY

Not long after their new monument had been completed, the Apprentice Boys faced a serious obstacle to the annual siege commemorations in the form of the passage in 1832 of the Party Processions Act, which prohibited all 'Orange' or 'Green' parades.[1] Neil Maddox has demonstrated that as a result of increased sectarian tensions and the violent conflicts that typically erupted during processions of a 'party' nature, particularly in Dublin, Armagh and Belfast, this new act 'represented the most extreme legislative response to contentious parading ever witnessed on the island of Ireland'.[2] Many liberal Protestants had been convinced that sectarian tensions would all but evaporate with Catholic emancipation in 1829, believing that the need for Catholic demonstrations as well as the ire behind Catholic opposition to Protestant marches would be lessened. However, Orange processions, particularly those organized by the Orange Order for the Twelfth of July – the anniversary of the Battle of the Boyne at which the forces of James II had been defeated in 1690 – continued to grow and to become more vituperative. Parading gave vent to loyalist anger at the loss of exclusive privileges, Maddox argues, and parliament eventually resorted to a total ban on all party-affiliated parades as a means to stem the tide.[3] With the banning of the Twelfth parades, rioting and disturbances followed in many heavily Protestant areas across the island that summer, and in Omagh an angry mob went so far as to burn an effigy of Edward Stanley, chief secretary of Ireland and the author of the unpopular bill.[4]

In Derry, locals offered arguments throughout the 1830s against the continuation of the siege celebrations, and even the *Ordnance Survey memoir* called them 'a cause of useless dissention'.[5] Nevertheless, the August 'Relief' celebrations went ahead exactly as planned. Artillery on the walls and inside them were fired at midnight, the cathedral bells rang all day long except during divine service and the Apprentice Boys assembled with prominent leaders of the city and enacted their procession to the cathedral, complete with an escort by the 30th Regiment and their full band, which played Orange melodies on both the outward and return journeys.[6] In December, the 'Shutting of the Gates' ceremony not only occurred despite the ban, but marked another – and extremely significant – shift of symbolic capital to the Walker Testimonial. And unlike the August commemorations, where the ordinary Protestants of Derry simply trailed along after the official procession and participated very little in official events, the new Party Processions Act would significantly affect the annual commemoration of the beginning of the siege, which had a parallel celebratory event for the general population.

Since at least the centenary commemorations of 1788, the December 'Shutting of the Gates' events sometimes included a ritual popular especially with the lower classes: the burning of a giant effigy of the 'traitor' Colonel Lundy, which in later times would have its chest packed with fireworks for greater effect. *Londonderry Journal* editor George Douglas, himself heavily involved in the centenary celebrations, writes of the event that after the official procession of prominent local men had concluded, a 'lower class of citizens' proceeded to march through the streets carrying an effigy of Lundy. They

2. *The burning of the effigy of Lundy, c.*1830.

then gathered in the Diamond and set it ablaze 'with every circumstance of ignominy'.[7] Although this constitutes the first mention of the burning of a figure of Lundy specifically in the historical record, the earliest siege commemorations in the wake of the relief itself took place within an existing type of street culture – a tradition of street theatre – which often centred on burnings in effigy of such figures as the pope and the Stuart 'pretender' James II.[8] It is not surprising, then, that following the siege, the figure of Lundy would eventually become the city's principal effigy. McBride rightly observes that unlike the more common effigy-burnings of Guy Fawkes throughout the three kingdoms and, later, the United Kingdom, the burning of Lundy in Derry has maintained its political significance into the present.[9] Little evidence exists that the tradition continued annually, but in light of the Party Processions Act, the practice again appears in the record in December 1832.

The *Londonderry Sentinel* chronicles the events of 18 December of that year. Early in the morning, the Apprentice Boys gathered and suspended the effigy of Lundy from the Corporation Hall in the Diamond. This suggests that, at least in some form, both the practice of burning a 'Lundy' and the location in which it occurred survived from the first recorded episode in 1788. We can reasonably suppose the practice to have continued to take place at least intermittently during the early part of the 19th century, as it is clear that the Apprentice Boys first attempted to proceed with their usual litany of ritual events on that day.[10] Indeed, the Ulster Museum in Belfast contains an oil painting on canvas by an unknown artist *c.*1830 (fig. 2) that depicts the traditional burning of the Lundy effigy from a cart in front of a public building not unlike the Corporation Hall.[11] On this occasion, however, sometime in the late morning the mayor ordered that the effigy be taken down, in accordance with the recent Party Processions Act. One might speculate that the more popular – and thus, more riotous and potentially volatile – event aroused more caution than the official procession of the Apprentice Boys and town elites, but the reason for the decision remains obscured. The situation apparently seemed so potentially inflammatory, however, that a group of policemen was stationed in front of the hall to prevent the re-erection and burning of the effigy. By noon, the figure of Lundy had been spirited away and taken instead to the Walker Testimonial, where it was suspended by rope from the platform at the top of the pillar and immediately set alight to the well-orchestrated accompaniment of 'Roaring Meg'.[12] This incident marks the first known burning of a Lundy effigy from Walker's pillar, and although it is clear that this had not been the original intention of the Apprentice Boys in charge of the day's festivities, it soon developed into one of their most symbolic traditions – and served to transfer yet another ritual, with its associated symbolism, to the site.

Despite the setbacks, and indeed the prosecution of several of the Apprentice Boys by the authorities as a result of their subterfuge, the siege commemorations continued and the annual processions remained a fixture in Derry civic life.[13] By 1845, the Party Processions Act had been allowed to lapse, but the conditions that prompted it were on the increase. Violent sectarian confrontations continued to plague the countryside as well as the towns of Ulster. One major skirmish saw the deaths of at least eight people during a clash between Orangemen and Ribbonmen at Dolly's Brae in Co. Down on the occasion of the Twelfth of July procession in 1849, which prompted the revival of the lapsed Processions Act the following year.[14] By the time of the major riots at Derrymacresh in Co. Armagh in 1860, a new bill began working its way through parliament during the Apprentice Boys' annual 'Relief' celebrations that year.[15] The Party Emblems Act had been designed to support the earlier ban on parading, and if passed, would now prohibit the playing of music in a public place, the discharging of firearms – including cannon – and the public display of banners or flags, all of which marked the traditional Orange celebrations across Ulster and especially those of the Apprentice Boys in Derry.[16] The bishop of Derry, also a member of the House of Lords and aware of the bill's progress, instructed the sexton of St Columb's not to allow the crimson flag to fly from its roof during the 'Relief' commemorations, nor to ring the bells. The Apprentice Boys raised the flag in defiance, nonetheless, prompting the bishop to send a curate to remove it, after which the loyalists immediately replaced it with another. The curate appealed to the local police, but the reply came that no law yet existed to interfere with

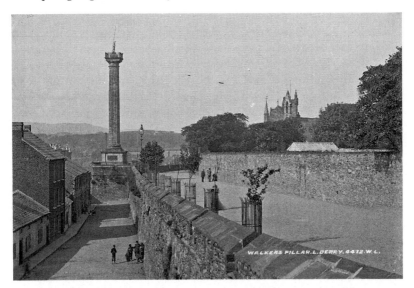

3. The Walker monument with its flagpole, late 19th century or early 20th century.
Source: National Library of Ireland, Lawrence Photograph Collection, L_CAB_04472.

the 'ancient usages of the city'.[17] Resistance to the efforts of authorities to curb the growing trend of sectarian violence across the region continued to rely heavily on appeals to 'tradition' and 'customary' ritual practice, indicating the prominence of these symbolic concepts within the loyalist tradition, and the siege narrative in particular. The Apprentice Boys of the mid-19th century lived within and continually reinforced a culture in which symbolism was prominent and the display of potentially divisive symbols highly controversial.

By December, the Party Emblems Act had passed, and the *Irish Times* special Derry correspondent reported that the Apprentice Boys found their 'Shutting of the Gates' ceremony attended by two government stipendiaries as well as 'two troops of the 3rd Light Dragoons, from Dundalk, under Captain Hobson; a detachment of the 86th foot, from Newry, commanded by Colonel Stewart; and Inspector-General Wood, with a large force of constabulary, amounting to between three and four hundred men'.[18] Evidence had reached the authorities that a counter-demonstration was being planned by Ribbonmen from Donegal. Nevertheless, despite the new legislation and a heavy police and military presence, the Apprentice Boys ramped up their ritual displays and, in the process, continued to transfer symbolic capital to the Walker Testimonial. In addition to the crimson flag on the cathedral steeple, they again hoisted the red city flag with 1688 emblazoned on its front to the top of Walker's pillar – as had become a new custom since its first display there in 1828 – and even placed a third flag on the top of Corporation Hall. They proceeded to hang the effigy of Lundy from the base of the monument, and several Apprentice Boys managed to drag a cannon to the walls just below its plinth and fire seven rounds before police finally intervened. All three prime symbols – flag, effigy, cannon – centred on the Walker pillar, and throughout the events 'the cavalry and constabulary were placed at various points around the city', but chose not to prevent the ritual displays despite their prohibition under the Party Emblems Act.[19] The Donegal Ribbonmen, and the threat of actual violence rather than symbolic display, seem to have been the real reason for the presence of such heavy force; yet the Catholic agitators never appeared and the banned commemorations proceeded peacefully, undisturbed.

The following August, John Hempton and 17 other men were summoned to account under the act in connection with their participation in the hoisting of the flag to the top of the Walker memorial and St Columb's cathedral during the 'Relief' celebrations, as well as for discharging cannon. The case was ultimately dismissed, and, as with the failure of the police and regiments to prevent the December celebrations, the influence of Orangeism on the local and regional authorities remained highly significant in the lack of prosecution of those engaged in prohibited displays.[20] In this period of high tensions and sectarian sentiment, the Walker monument became firmly established as a pivotal element and symbolic location in both the December and August siege commemorations.

The last few years of the 1860s raised tensions to altogether new heights, and it is here we find some of the strongest evidence for the increased symbolic role of the Walker pillar. At one end of the Irish political spectrum, the Fenian movement for national independence was on the rise, and had gained much publicity with its involvement surrounding the affair of the so-called 'Manchester Martyrs' – three Fenians hanged in the English city for their role in the death of a local policemen during an attempted escape – in 1867. At the other, the stalwart Orangeman William Johnstone actively lobbied for the repeal of the prohibitive acts of 1845 and 1860. Johnstone even landed himself in jail for a month's stay when he organized a massive Orange procession from Newtownards to Bangor in direct defiance of those same acts.[21] Of even greater significance, however, were changes that stemmed from the 1868 general election, in which the Liberal party secured a victory and promptly proceeded to disestablish the Church of Ireland. As a result of the Reform Act issued the previous year, the number of enfranchised Catholics had expanded dramatically, and in Derry they had formed an alliance with the Presbyterian Liberals in order to secure a seat in parliament for their candidate and indeed succeeded in ousting the Conservative incumbent. McBride observes that over the next three years, 'a series of clashes occurred between the Apprentice Boys, and the "Bogside" or "Catholic" party, beginning with an attack on a Liberal meeting by an armed Protestant mob on 20 July 1868'.[22] This climate set the stage for a series of contentious public displays unlike those the city had witnessed thus far.

The setting for the most disastrous event of the decade, however, was not one of the annual siege events, but instead a visit to Derry by Queen Victoria's son, Prince Arthur, in the spring of 1869. In spite of the difference of occasion, the Apprentice Boys greeted the prince in the manner in which they were well-versed – by parading, this time with their recently organized Britannia Flute Band, and firing a 21-gun salute in his majesty's honour. The rival Hibernia Flute Band, a Catholic group, also played for the prince and organized a procession through the city in which they carried a green flag with a harp (but no crown) and called for an 'Irish republic'. Clashes inevitably ensued, three men were shot dead, and a crown commission of enquiry had to be established to determine the causes of the unfortunate incidents that marred the royal visit.[23] The commission highlighted the Apprentice Boys' annual siege commemorations as a particular cause of tension within the city generally, and the report notes their role with remarkable clarity.

> [To] heighten the difficulty of the case, the city of their common habitation is one, whose heroic defence, at the time of that civil conflict, is the proudest recollection of the one section, while its celebration, for the other, is identified with the memory of not only the reverses and the ruin which befell their side in the struggle, but with that of long-after days of bitter humiliation.[24]

Indeed, such a description would adequately convey the divisions in the city still today. One witness for the commission testified that 'we shall never have peace in this city', while another asserted that 'there is a very bad feeling towards the Apprentice Boys, and there has been for thirty years'.[25] In total, the commission's report marks the first official government identification of the Derry siege commemorations as a prime source of civil strife in the city.

One of the two principal witnesses on behalf of the organization itself was the local architect John Fergusson, whose defence of the celebrations is noteworthy as a strategy of narrative mythologizing. Fergusson asserted, contrary to the statement of the witness above, that there existed in Derry no longstanding malice against the Apprentice Boys or their parades, yet the rest of his testimony clearly indicates that the organization saw itself as being under threat from a rival perspective, and his assertions are full of defensive language. He claimed the Apprentice Boys 'would all lose their lives before they would give up their celebrations ... because I think that if everything is yielded, even the right to meet and celebrate an event, other demands will have to be met – perhaps the wall itself taken down shortly or Walker's Pillar'.[26] This last conjecture suggests much about Fergusson's object. A defence against the prohibitive processions acts would naturally include the organization's traditional interest in commemorating the siege, but the static, stone symbols of the siege mythology itself – the walls of the city, and now, tellingly,

Walker's pillar – were controversial only within the local sectarian narratives of triumphalism. Their continued existence remained unaffected by the Party Processions and Party Emblems Acts, but in the eyes of the man chosen to represent the Apprentice Boys to the commission, they too were under attack. In this context, the Walker memorial had developed within the narrative to hold as much importance as a symbolic object as the unbreached walls of the city themselves. As we will explore in greater depth later in the chapter, mythologizing narratives served to transfer symbolic capital to the pillar just as effectively as physical ritual processes.

The circumstances of the siege celebrations of the next two years would again result in the reinforcement of the monument's position as the city's central symbol. Prompted by the events of the spring of 1869, the Catholic Workingmen's Liberal Defence Association had formed in opposition to the Apprentice Boys. That December, in preparation for a tense commemorative event, 1,500 troops and 750 additional police arrived in the city, although Milligan asserts that this was merely 'to assure protection to the Apprentice Boys from the Bogsiders and [other] contingents from Inishowen who wanted to prevent the procession'.[27] There was no repeat of the spring's violence, but the following summer the new Workingmen's Association planned to hold a rival parade and demonstration rather than to prevent the 'Relief' parade. These plans occasioned the presence of 1,000 police, six companies of the North Devon Regiment, and a squadron of Dragoon Guards in Derry city.[28] Fraser notes that although excursion trains from Belfast were banned for the day, two flute bands from Coleraine managed to enter the city via the regular service and that by all accounts 'the exuberance of their playing added to the tensions of the day'. Later in the day, when the bands returned to the station for their journey home, they were met by a large, hostile crowd and shots were fired, leading to a disturbance that could only be quelled by the mayor reading the Riot Act and by several cavalry charges.[29] This incident led to the magistrates issuing a ban on the burning of all effigies in the city during the month of December 1870, and occasioned one of the most decisive events in support of the Walker Testimonial's position of primacy in the siege mythology.

Once again, large contingents of police and military entered the city 'to prevent the burning of Lundy', scheduled to occur on Sunday, 18 December. As it happened, however, the preassembled effigy of the traitor mysteriously went missing during the night of Thursday, 15 December. The Apprentice Boys' search for the missing Lundy proceeded all day Friday and continued unsuccessfully into Saturday while, in the meantime, police cut off all public access to Walker's pillar, from which the effigy was due to be suspended. Further, the Apprentice Boys placed placards throughout the city on Saturday announcing their postponement of the effigy burning 'for the present', due to the 'illegal and unconstitutional action of the partisan magistrates of Derry, backed by an overwhelming military and police force, supplied by a benevolent

Government'.[30] At an emergency meeting held Saturday evening, the leadership of the organization appointed a delegation tasked with approaching the walls and demanding access to the Walker Testimonial in order to hoist the flag for the anniversary of the shutting of the gates. Milligan records that they discovered a strong contingent of police stationed immediately in front of the pillar and that all access for any purpose continued to be denied.[31]

Having been thus thwarted in their original plan by force of arms – and indeed at least two members attempted to push through the police lines unsuccessfully – the Apprentice Boys celebrated their anniversary on Sunday, 18 December with as many of the usual ritual elements as they could manage: the firing of cannon, the ringing of the cathedral bells, and the hoisting of the crimson flag to the cathedral steeple, which had not been guarded. Then, appearing as normal as possible, they proceeded to march down Bishop Street, which was still lined with police, and assembled in the Corporation Hall to enact their hasty back-up plan. The *Derry Journal* reports that the celebrants occupied the hall for the rest of the day 'with continuous fifing and drumming'.[32] The police responded by surrounding the hall on all sides. Then, in a surprising twist, an effigy of Lundy – having been recovered or reconstructed in the interval since Thursday evening – was suddenly 'launched from the top of the hall and set ablaze', prompting police finally to burst into the hall with bayonets pointed. As a final gesture, the Apprentice Boys had pinned to Lundy's chest the proclamation banning the burning of all effigies in the city of Derry.[33]

This incident marks a clear contrast with the 'Shutting of the Gates' celebrations of December, 1832. At both events, access to the preferred venue for the burning of the Lundy effigy was denied by police blockade and, on both occasions, the Apprentice Boys found an alternative location to effect the blaze. Crucially, however, the role of the Walker Testimonial had switched with that of the Corporation Hall between 1832 and 1870. By the latter date, the Testimonial undoubtedly had become the 'traditional' site for the inferno, likely bolstered by the annual repetition of the ritual at that location. Such repetition of ritual – and with it, repeated transfer and affirmation of symbolic value – is unlikely to have occurred at the Corporation Hall for very many years between the first effigy-burning in 1788 and the date in 1832 when the ritual moved to the Walker pillar. By 1870, the Walker Testimonial had been the preferred site for decades, and *it* was the location the police blockaded, not the hall as they had done in 1832. And just as in that year, the Apprentice Boys first attempted to gain access to their preferred locale, even in the absence of the effigy itself, before resorting to staging the burning at their back-up location. The contentious events of the decade had solidified the status of the Walker memorial as the symbol at the very centre of the local loyalist tradition.

Although clashes continued sporadically throughout the succeeding decades, the tensions of the late 1860s – at least as they concerned the Derry siege celebrations – would not be matched again for nearly a century. The

'Relief' and 'Shutting of the Gates' celebrations were banned outright for a year
following the disturbances of 1870, and police again occupied the Walker pillar
on the commemoration days of 1871 just to be sure the events did not go ahead.
Significant disturbances did occur in 1883, but not during the bicentenary
celebrations of 1888–9. The so-called 'nationalization' of Irish politics at the end
of the 19th century and the continued separation of religious communities –
and especially Protestant understanding of their increasing minority position –
ensured that political and social tensions remained a fixture in Ireland, but for a
time at least, the outward manifestations of these tensions focused on Dublin,
the island's political centre, and Belfast, its commercial and industrial hub in the
north. Meanwhile, however, the transactional processes of transferring symbolic
capital to the Walker monument continued in other forms.

THE MYTH OF THE SWORD

Physical interactions between the people of Derry and the embodied symbols in
their landscape form one type of archive for the investigation of the processes of
symbolic conflict. Equally important, however, are the strategies for developing
and propagating the narratives and myths that also serve to bolster one side or
another in struggles for social and cultural dominance. In the context of the
Derry siege commemorations, the Walker Testimonial, as we have already
begun to see, began to take on significance in local narratives as well as its new
physical role in the ritual processes of commemorations in the local calendar.
The establishment of one myth in particular, and the enmeshing of certain
symbols within that myth, had the effect of transferring symbolic capital to
the Walker Testimonial just as surely as the burning of the Lundy effigy at the
physical site. This myth – that the statue of Walker at the very top of the pillar
originally held a sword – remains so powerful that it continues to be spread
today, among historians and locals alike. Investigating this myth, its origins and
its falsity, will provide a window into the narrative form of symbolic conflict
and the transfer of symbolic capital it entails.

Local tradition maintains that Walker's statue held a sword in its left hand
when it was originally erected, but that it was lost during a particularly intense
storm. Variations of the myth abound, but the most common is that which is
repeated by Ian McBride in his 1997 history of the siege commemorations – that
the sword 'was blown down in a storm, as local tradition has it, on the day that
Catholic emancipation passed'. McBride cites the similar claim of the celebrated
travel writer, actor, and singer Richard Hayward in his 1938 popular history, *In
praise of Ulster*, as evidence for this tradition.[34] Such a detail may seem trivial, but
it is important to ask, especially when a narrative tradition endures for as long as
this one, what work a myth like this is doing in its cultural context, and for the
benefit of whom? The actual truth of the presence of the sword itself remains

secondary in this case, as the important feature of the myth is the association of the fall of the sword with the advent of Catholic emancipation. For Catholics, perpetuating a myth like this suggests the perception of a zero-sum conflict: a success for us is a failure for our rivals, i.e., an increase in Catholic fortunes occasions a decrease in the status of Protestantism, and that decrease is neatly represented symbolically by the stripping away of a symbol of power and authority – a sword – from the most prominent symbol of Protestantism in the Derry landscape. For loyalists, keeping such a narrative alive has the effect of suggesting that the erosion of Protestant privileges, as represented by the loss of Walker's sword on the night of Catholic emancipation, remains a real threat with an established historical precedent, and a threat that must be guarded against in the future. Associating this threat with the Walker monument assures the monument's position as integral to the symbolic fight against the perceived loss of Protestant status.

However, there is no contemporary evidence for the presence of a sword in the hand of the original statue. As we have seen, the statue was raised to its position in August 1828, just a few months before George IV signed his name to the Roman Catholic Relief Act in the spring of 1829. While it would not have been impossible for a sword to have been present for these few months, there is no record of it either in the *Londonderry Journal* reports of the dedication of the statue or in the *Ordnance Survey memoir*, the writer of which was present at the ceremony. Further, it is difficult to imagine how such a sword could have been held in the grip of the statue's left hand – its right has always held a Bible – when the fingers were undoubtedly arranged into a pointing gesture, as evidenced in numerous photographs and drawings prior to its initial destruction in the 1970s, as well as by the eminent British historian and politician, Thomas Babington Macaulay. The first volume of Macaulay's monumental and immensely popular *History of England from the succession of James the Second* appeared in 1848 and gives one of the most famous and laudatory descriptions of the city and the siege of Derry. Macaulay notes the position of the hand of the Walker statue upon his visit to the city in the early 1840s. His description of the monument is worth noting in its entirety as it captures many of the Protestant sentiments of the period:

> Five generations have since passed away; and still the wall of Londonderry is to the Protestants of Ulster what the trophy of Marathon was to the Athenians. A lofty pillar, rising from a bastion which bore during many weeks the heaviest fire of the enemy, is seen far up and far down the Foyle. On the summit is the statue of Walker, such as when, in the last and most terrible emergency, his eloquence roused the fainting courage of his brethren. In one hand he grasps a Bible. The other, pointing down the river, seems to direct the eyes of his famished audience to the English topmasts in the distant bay. Such a monument was well deserved: yet it

was scarcely needed: for in truth the whole city is to this day a monument
of the great deliverance.[35]

Macaulay's account was incredibly well-received and circulated astonishingly
widely in its day, and the accuracy of his observation did not attract comment
at the time, which would have been likely had he been mistaken. For many, in
fact, his account was given credibility 'by his willingness to pace the ground, for
he took the trouble to visit the city'.[36] If the original myth was true, however,
Macaulay's failure to observe a sword would be consistent with its having
disappeared more than a decade prior to his arrival in the city. But the most
striking evidence for the lack of an original sword is provided by an illustration
of the memorial on the frontispiece of John Graham's history of the siege,
the preface of which is dated January, 1829 – three months before the king
signed the emancipation act – and which depicts the statue without a sword.[37]
With such evidence to the contrary, what accounts for the development and
persistence of the sword myth among not only local residents, but generations
of modern commentators such as Hayward and McBride? Where and how did
this narrative originate?

A significant contributing factor may have been the numerous depictions of
the governor carrying a sword in his left hand that appear in paintings located
in the city for centuries, including one that used to hang on the Butcher's Street
wall of the Corporation Hall in the Diamond,[38] and several appearing in the
Chapter House of St Columb's cathedral. That residents and visitors to the city
would have had visual access to both the pillar and the paintings is suggested
by the traveller's account of the famous progenitor of the Mellon family of
Pittsburgh, Pennsylvania, and founder of Mellon Bank, Thomas Mellon. Mellon
had been born in Co. Tyrone before emigrating with his family to Pennsylvania
in 1818, and as such would have been more familiar with the siege mythology
than an American-born traveller. His account mirrors that of Macaulay in
several of its details, but with one major exception. Mellon travelled to Derry
in 1882, many years after Macaulay, yet he notes that the statue – the subject of
which he incorrectly identifies as 'John' Walker – 'still keeps one hand on the
open Bible whilst he grasps a sword with the other, on the summit of his tower:
a shining example of the former force of religious opinion'.[39] This account
appears in Mellon's autobiography, which he composed primarily for the use
of his family and left unpublished, and therefore it cannot be considered to
have contributed to the popularity of the myth, but it does raise an interesting
possibility. The composition of Mellon's account, presumably from memory
as he mentions no notes or journals, contains an obvious error of recollection
of Walker's name, referring to him as John instead of George, and it is likely
that this faulty recollection also accounts for the inaccuracy of his portrayal
of the monument. Further, Mellon relates that he also visited St Columb's
cathedral, where he most likely viewed the portraits of Walker with his Bible

and sword in hand, perhaps influencing his later recollection.[40] Such portrayals of Walker remained accessible in Derry and they still comprise the majority of representations of the clerical warrior today, potentially still lending credibility to the myth of the sword.

Mellon may have had another, less innocent, reference point for aiding his memory in the form of the highly partisan account of the Irish nationalist and, later, Canadian politician Thomas D'Arcy McGee, whose description of the monument in his *Popular history of Ireland* likely generated the myth. McGee's work culminated in a narrative of the arrival of Catholic emancipation and he affords the following anecdote the honour of concluding his monumental, two-volume study. The narrative no doubt serves to highlight the significance of emancipation and the perceived ultimate downfall of Protestantism:

> A lofty column of the walls of Derry bore the effigy of Bishop Walker,[41] who fell at the Boyne, armed with a sword, typical of his martial inclinations, rather than of his religious calling. Many long years, by day and night, had his sword, sacred to liberty or ascendency, according to the eyes with which the spectator regarded it, turned its steadfast point to the broad estuary of Loch Foyle. Neither wintry storms nor summer rains had loosened it in the grasp of the warlike churchman's effigy, until, on the 13th day of April, 1829 – the day the royal signature was given to the Act of Emancipation – the sword of Walker fell with a prophetic crash upon the ramparts of Derry, and was shattered to pieces. So, we may now say, without bitterness and almost without reproach, so may fall and shiver to pieces, every code, in every land beneath the sun, which impiously attempts to shackle conscience, or endows an exclusive caste with the rights and franchises which belong to an entire People![42]

Despite the obvious chronological flaws in McGee's unsubstantiated account, it displays all the hallmarks of the myth still so recently reported by McBride and lingering in certain quarters of Derry. This variety of narrative mythologizing deploys a type of rhetoric that not only is not without malice, but which also performs considerable symbolic work in its coupling of embodied objects with national mythic significance. McGee's is the earliest such account, published in 1869, and the likeliest candidate responsible for the propagation of the sword mythology. Surviving contemporary (and later) portraits accessible for viewing in the city's Anglican cathedral and its town hall serve to provide 'corroboration' for the story, while the appeal to the nationalist tradition of the symbolic triumph of emancipation above and beyond its actual, legal ramifications, remains powerful. These elements have filtered down to the present day and continue to fuel the narratives of division that keep the Walker memorial in controversy. That the monument should be the locus of such a powerful and longstanding mythic and symbolic tradition, especially among Catholics, demonstrates its continued central importance among the symbols of loyalism in the city of Derry.

This chapter has traced the increasing symbolic importance attached to the Walker Testimonial through several tumultuous decades of the mid-19th century, both in the mythological and public commemorative arenas. The rhetoric and longevity of the myth of the sword suggests that the monument accrued enough symbolic power to sustain a counterfactual myth from its likely nationalist origins through to the scholarship of the present. The appeal of such a triumphalist account, as it turns out to be, and one itself mirroring the loyalist narratives it opposes, held staying power due to the standing of the memorial as the prime target within the symbolic landscape of loyalism. The often violent and uproarious history of the century's siege commemorations, and particularly the burning of the Lundies, serves to reveal the processes through which the monument accrued such capital as the decades wore on. The continued and persistent locating by the Apprentice Boys of important commemorative elements of their celebrations at the site of the memorial, coupled with the narrative mythologizing evident in contemporary accounts of events, such as that of Fergusson, as well as in the persistent sword myth, collectively raised the profile of the pillar and contributed to the tensions already at work in the city.

The symbolic power embodied in the memorial would come to reach its pinnacle through a set of additional, though vastly more costly, commemorative and reactionary episodes in the mid-20th century. As physical confrontations involving the Walker Testimonial became infrequent after the tense decades of the previous century, narratives rife with symbolic triumphalism continued to abound. In such a cauldron as Derry became during the Troubles, these underlying tensions bubbled so violently that the explosion of intense conflict that followed seemed all but inevitable. However, the vastly complex historical context requires that our analysis should take into account the shifting role of the symbolic landscape in an era in which the initial causes of tension surrounding the Walker memorial became largely forgotten, and in which the symbolic tradition itself took over in primary importance. The next chapter will explore the ways in which the people of Derry attempted the use the pillar to engage in symbolic conflict during the Troubles, and in the following period of identity politicking that still obtains in the city today.

3. The monument during the Troubles

Between 2013 and 2015, a visitor to the Apprentice Boys' Memorial Hall and museum would have been greeted upon entering by Governor George Walker. For nearly two years, the statue occupied a position just inside the doorway of the public entrance to the museum, with its imposing size all the more dominating at ground level. Its head and pointing left arm were new, as were portions of the legs and chest, and large seams bound the parts of its unshattered original torso and other bodily fragments to its new appendages, but the governor was unmistakable. The image of a reconstituted Walker, proudly standing at the entrance to the museum dedicated to the organization responsible for his commemoration, suggested both historical rupture and continuity, a binding of old and new, and a vision that encompassed both. The statue stood as a visible marker of loyalist commitment to their traditional narrative – fractured and adapted, but not destroyed: its very cracks and seams symbolic of its endurance and indestructibility. This situation was short-lived. By late 2015, the statue had been replastered in its entirety, covering up any traces of its vulnerability and proclaiming its dominance from the top of a new pedestal, visible high up from the street level through a purpose-built display window on the second floor of its new museum, funded by a grant of more than £2 million from the European Union. The fortunes of the Walker statue reveal to a considerable degree those of the loyalist narrative that sustains it, and together they form the subject of this final chapter.

By the late 19th century, the Walker Testimonial stood as one of the primary symbols of Derry loyalism and the political power wielded by its adherents in the city. As the siege celebrations continued throughout the 20th century, the monument's reputation was maintained, and the outbreak of the Troubles situated it at the very heart of the city's pantheon of loyalist symbols. Taking the destruction of the statue in 1973 as its central event, this chapter explores the context in which the memorial was obliterated from the city's physical landscape. During the Troubles, the siege commemorations occupied a critical position in the struggle for political power in Derry, and the escalating violence and agitation surrounding the events of Bloody Sunday in 1972 lent further significance to the display of loyalist symbols in the now largely Catholic, largely nationalist city. Examining these events, their origins, and the following repeated cycle of destruction, repair and rededication that attached to the statue of Walker himself reveals the degree to which the processes and strategies of commemoration and narrativization have embedded the memorial in the permanent plane of symbolic conflict in contemporary Derry.

THE EARLY 20TH CENTURY AND THE BUILD-UP TO THE TROUBLES

The early part of the century saw little of the type of conflict so prevalent in the late 1860s. The Apprentice Boys' siege celebrations continued in their 'traditional' forms, however, including the burning of the effigy of Lundy at the Walker pillar. The ritual had become such a common feature of annual Derry loyalist practice that it was even replicated on the Western Front by members of the Ulster Division, who orchestrated a procession accompanied by Orange tunes and followed by the burning of two homemade Lundies in December of 1915, while the official celebrations proceeded back at home.[1] By the end of the war, the landslide victory of Sinn Féin to take control of Derry Corporation in 1918 marked the first time that unionists had lost formal power in the city, and tensions began to mount afresh. Shortly thereafter, the War of Independence broke out in the south, and throughout the next two years, the majority of fighting took place in the south of Ireland between Irish revolutionary forces and the British state authorities. By 1920, fighting had reached the north, although it was largely characterized instead by sectarian clashes, many of which occurred in Derry in the summer of that year when at least 40 people were killed.[2] That December, the city remained under a corporation proclamation that prohibited all processions, yet the Apprentice Boys managed to secure permission to burn a Lundy with less than the usual pomp and circumstance from their own Memorial Hall, rather than suspended from the customary and provocative Walker pillar.[3]

The celebrations carried on throughout the Irish Civil War and Second World War, with familiar tensions dying down and the unionists reclaiming control of the corporation. A curious incident in the spring of 1951, however, highlights both the ongoing symbolic importance of the Walker pillar as well as the level of relative calm in the city at the time. On Easter Sunday, the 35th anniversary of the Easter Rising of 1916, the sun rose over Derry to reveal the Irish tricolour flying from the hand of Governor Walker atop his promontory.[4] During the previous night, according to the *Ulster Herald*, local 'republicans daringly forced an entrance to the base of the obelisk [sic] while a dance was being held in the Apprentice Boys' Hall a few yards away, climbed in the darkness to the summit, and placed the Tricolour firmly in position waving over the city'.[5] On their way back out, the unknown pranksters replaced the lock with a more complex version in order to prolong the amount of time their banner could fly. Police eventually broke through in the morning and removed the offending flag, but not before 'hundreds of citizens gathered in amazement to watch what they had never seen before'. The paper reports, unsurprisingly, that 'the Derry Orangemen are very angry', and this distress apparently filtered across the Irish Sea, for 'not even the disappearance of the Stone of Scone aroused as much anger in Westminster Abbey as has the appearance of the Tricolour on the Walls'. However, the reaction within the city itself is most telling: 'Local unionist newspapers are trying to whip up general public indignation but citizen reaction is one of intense amusement at the way in which the Orange element was caught out.'[6]

This sentiment undoubtedly represents the feelings of the nationalist majority, and the jocular nature of the incident is to be assured. Nevertheless, the episode may also be interpreted as a valuation contest in a field of symbolic conflict. Such a contest, which involves the 'ranking of symbols of the competing groups' identities', can take either positive or negative forms, and in the tricolour incident we see both varieties. According to Simon Harrison, the 'negative tactic is directed at the symbols of the opposition and consists simply in attempts to diminish their status', while positive efforts increase the corresponding status of one's own symbols.[7] This, in many ways, is precisely what we see occurring at Easter, 1951. The 'republicans' temporarily appropriated the highest symbol in the loyalist repertoire for the purposes of positively raising the status, symbolic capital and quite literally the position of their own flag, while negatively affecting the credibility and symbolic potency of the Walker memorial. In a zero-sum contest such as this, a perception exists such that a move up the sliding scale of value for one group's identity markers or status symbols forces a corresponding move down the scale for the opposition.[8] That such a contest proceeded with very little tension, and no open or violent confrontation speaks to the situation of relative calm that obtained in the city at the time. In the absence of widespread political conflict, the stakes in 1951 were relatively low. Nevertheless, the conflict over symbolism had not disappeared.

Similar acts of nonviolent contestation appear within the narrative mythological corpus surrounding the memorial as well. Much like in the earlier period of physical confrontation, narrativization and historical mythologizing continued to play a significant role in the ongoing, albeit low-level, conflict over the city's iconography. One such common narrative is still repeated today, and runs more or less as follows. When the Apprentice Boys would gather at the Walker Testimonial for their December 'Shutting of the Gates' celebration, the Catholic families who lived in the houses right below the old city walls on the outside of the old town would attempt to subvert the celebrations by lighting their coal fires. As one prominent local figure who grew up in the nationalist community put it, 'They were always hoping for a windy day, and the wind blowing up towards the walls, and they would light a fire and make sure the fire was smoky so that the smoke would drift up.'[9] Much the same as the tricolour incident, these efforts suggest that people had almost settled into patterns of behaviour in which nonviolent display and resistance won the day. While stories such as this are often oral transmissions, they do occasionally also appear in print. Seamus Deane, for instance, in his novel *Reading in the dark*, evokes a similar sense of passivity and settled resistance in his description of the December ceremony. In a chapter entitled 'Lundy burns', Deane describes how smoke would rise up from the chimneys of the houses below the walls while 'Lundy, the traitor,

4. Chimneys at the base of the monument, late 19th or early 20th century.
Source: National Library of Ireland, Lawrence Collection, L_CAB_04475.

swung always on the hero's pillar, a hanged giant, exploding in flame to the roll of drums from the massed bands below'.[10] In this context, the smoke becomes another symbol in the repertoire of conflict, a voiceless objection to the effigy, the bands and the 'hero's pillar' that dominated the day. This discourse of resistance, however calm, nonetheless served to keep the proverbial as well as the actual coal fires of the nationalist community burning.

This period of relative calm surrounding the Walker monument and the siege celebrations would be short-lived. By 1968, agitation for civil rights for Catholics in the city had mounted. Bernadette Devlin, civil rights campaigner and later the UK's youngest woman MP, dubbed the heavily gerrymandered Derry 'the capital city of injustice' for its overt discrimination against Catholics, particularly in terms of housing and employment. Civil rights demonstrators that year came up against violent opposition from the Royal Ulster Constabulary (RUC) as well as elements of Derry's loyalist hard line. Tensions during the following summer were riding extremely high in the run-up to the Apprentice Boys' annual march for the 'Relief' celebration, which had by then acquired a new 'traditional' element – a march around the city's walls, which took them past Catholic territory in the area below the bastion known as the Bogside. The RUC had previously carried out violent incursions into the Bogside in both January and April of 1969, and as the Apprentice Boys' parade approached, the residents of the area prepared for confrontation. On the day of the anniversary commemoration, as the members of the organization marched past the Bogside, clashes erupted between Catholic residents of the area and the RUC. The

Apprentice Boys' procession kicked off three days of fighting that culminated in the presence of the British army on the streets. This confrontation, televised around the world, became known as the Battle of the Bogside, and with it, the Troubles had begun in Derry in earnest.

Thus, having been firmly associated with the outbreak of violence in the city, both of the annual Apprentice Boys marches were banned outright for the next two years. However, the organization still found a way to utilize its biggest and most visible symbol. Outside of Derry, the most important date in the Orange calendar is the Twelfth of July, not August, in honour of the victory of King William III over the forces of the ousted Catholic King James II at the Battle of the Boyne in 1690. This commemorative event, although celebrated by loyalists across Northern Ireland, had been often overshadowed in Derry by the two dates of more significance in their local calendar. In July of 1970, however, with the ban firmly in place on their August commemorations, the Apprentice Boys seized the opportunity to utilize the Walker Testimonial in a new fashion.

On the afternoon of the Twelfth, members of the group climbed to the top of the pillar and decorated the statue of Walker in an Orange sash (long the symbol of the Orange Order) and gave him an Orange flag to hold in his pointing left hand, much in the manner he had held the tricolour on the republican anniversary in 1951. The base of the plinth they decorated on all its four sides with banners emblazoned with the names of the four great battles in the Protestant tradition – Boyne, Derry, Enniskillen and Aughrim.[11] A large military guard was stationed along the wall near the memorial, and the soldiers both permitted the decoration to remain and tolerated a small march in which approximately 500 Apprentice Boys proceeded to the Carlisle Road Presbyterian Church, about a quarter-mile from the walls overlooking the Bogside.[12] Again we may see in this incident another valuation contest for the pillar's ultimate symbolic status. The Apprentice Boys made a powerful statement of their control of the iconographic landscape, while the Catholic population immediately below the walls was reminded of the political domination of the minority unionist position within the city. It is of particular significance here that this marks the first important occasion on which the Walker Testimonial's symbolic capital – generated almost entirely from siege mythology – was utilized for the wider, non-siege-specific Orange cause. The use of the pillar and its plinth established both that the Apprentice Boys were still able to stage commemorative events in spite of the official ban on their usual days of ceremony, and that their preferred location remained the Walker monument regardless of the occasion. It would be in this context of expanding symbolic and political conflict that events would ultimately unfold to bring down Walker's pillar.

THE BOMBING OF THE PILLAR AND ITS MYTHOLOGY

As the political and military situation in Derry became increasingly violent over the succeeding year, including the start of a significant IRA campaign, the Northern Irish government ratcheted the turmoil up yet another notch. As many political observers had long anticipated, a policy of internment without trial was instituted on 9 August 1971, and hundreds were arrested in pre-dawn raids. It was against this background that the Northern Ireland Civil Rights Association launched a protest march on 30 January 1972, which would end in tragedy. Members of the British army's First Battalion, Parachute Regiment, opened fire on the civil rights protesters and bystanders, shooting 26 people and killing 13. A further victim died later in hospital. The event, which became known as 'Bloody Sunday', galvanized the nationalists of Derry. As violence continued throughout that year, the Apprentice Boys planned a less intrusive march in August – in spite of the ban on their commemorative activities that remained in place through the end of the year – during which they would confine themselves largely to the predominantly Protestant Waterside area of the city. Tensions in the city remained too high to run any risk of open conflict, however, and the organization ultimately cancelled the 'Relief' celebrations of 1973 altogether.

By the time the following August arrived, there had been no siege celebration at the Walker Testimonial for four years, but it towered nonetheless over the Bogside, and, with the Troubles in full swing, remained a prominent symbol of loyalism. While it remains unclear whether any specific event prompted the destruction of the monument later that month, the days preceding the bombing were highly charged. On 21 August, the government finally produced the long-awaited results of its official enquiry into the events of Bloody Sunday – the Widgery report. Despite the recommendation of Major Hubert O'Neill, the Derry coroner in charge of the inquest, that the British army was guilty of 'sheer, unadulterated murder', the inquest jury returned an open verdict, effectively absolving the army and the government of any guilt.[13] Emotions ran high in both communities in the wake of the report. The volatile unionist figurehead Revd Ian Paisley, by this time a member of parliament for North Antrim, announced that 'Mr O'Neill is not fit to be coroner for he has let his religious and political feelings dictate his decision', and stated also that he would ask the Northern Ireland secretary for Major O'Neill's dismissal.[14] Meanwhile, reactions and protests in the nationalist and republican communities abounded, and it remains a distinct possibility that this long-awaited, and ultimately highly unsatisfactory result may have had a part in prompting the bombing of the city's most prominent loyalist symbol just a few days later.

The details of the bombing itself remain mostly obscured, but the narrative we can piece together runs as follows. At midnight on 27 August, police were informed that a bomb was about to detonate on Magazine Street, a small street

5. Soldier at the base of the bombed pillar, 27 Aug 1973. © Victor Patterson.

near the Walker Testimonial, inside the city walls. The police responded and the area was duly cleared. As announced, at a few minutes past midnight, a bomb containing approximately 100 pounds of a substance like gelignite detonated at the pillar.[15] Reports from the scene indicated that very little damage resulted around the vicinity of the monument. A 30-foot section of the railing at St Augustine's church – some 20 yards from the memorial – was ripped away and deposited among the headstones of the churchyard, yet none of the church's windows were broken.[16] A stump of Walker's column measuring about 7 feet remained at the base of the plinth, which was itself largely undamaged, while the statue of the governor himself fell almost straight down and rested on its back on top of the plinth. Pieces of chain and rope were found nearby the pillar, which led police to believe that the bombers climbed up 25 feet over the wall to the memorial's base from the Bogside below, and they further suspected that the bomb had been placed outside the pillar rather than inside on the stairway (as had been the case with the destruction of Nelson's pillar in Dublin in 1966).[17]

Not long after the bombing, the Provisional IRA issued a statement in which they claimed the destruction and announced: 'The monument was built in defiance of the nationally-minded people of Derry and served as a symbol of unionist domination. Once again we have demonstrated our ability to strike at the enemy when and where we choose.'[18] This outright recognition of the monument's standing as a 'symbol of unionist domination' and the IRA's insistence that they held as their intended purpose, at least in part, to demonstrate their 'ability to strike at the enemy' in the manner of their own

choosing, confirms the act as a deliberate symbolic contest in the iconographic
landscape of the city. This time, however, rather than another valuation contest,
in which the status of a symbol moves along a sliding scale of relative value, this
effort may be seen as an escalated mode of conflict – an expansionary contest
– in which a rival group's symbols are destroyed or obliterated. In this type of
conflict, according to Harrison, a given group 'tries to displace its rivals' symbols
of identity', which can result in 'the disappearance of the defeated side's identity
symbols'.[19] The political function of a symbol destroyed in this way, therefore,
alters dramatically as a result of the 'expansionary contest'. The midnight blast
on Derry's ancient walls occasioned the immediate removal, after 145 years, of
what had become the most symbolically charged icon in the city's landscape.
By removing this imposing figure of unionist political domination and loyalist
cultural tradition, the anonymous bombers succeeded in striking at the heart of
their opposition's symbolic identity and obliterating its most precious icon.

This reading – and Harrison's model – falls short of encompassing the full
historical and cultural reality of the event. However useful the obliteration
narrative may be in understanding the motivation for such an attack, it is
important to remember that the cultural importance of the monument didn't
simply disappear overnight. The limestone may have vanished from the
bastion on that night in August 1973, and its immediate political function
may have decreased to almost nil, but much of the symbolic capital that had
for so long accrued within the memorial lived on in its prolific mythology,
propagated by both the unionist *and* nationalist communities. Much as it
had during the monument's tenure on the city walls, narrative myth-making
retained its significance in the cultural milieu that accompanied the Troubles.
The monument became reinterpreted, its capital appropriated. Some remained
with the Apprentice Boys, as we shall see, and some indeed became the cultural
property of nationalists. A new, parallel symbol, for instance, now exists and
holds currency with that community below the walls. A stained-glass window
located in a popular pub, The Bogside Inn, immortalizes the pillar's destruction
with the simple glass lettering '12:03' – the time of the blast.

Both groups continued to struggle over claims of possession of the physical
monument itself. One popular anecdote holds that pieces of the Testimonial,
and especially the statue of Walker, were collected by the Catholic residents of
the Bogside below the site of the blast and kept as souvenirs. It is difficult to
track the pervasiveness of this myth today, but the claim still circulated 40 years
later on the web pages and blogs of the unionist community. Alan Day, then
webmaster of the popular website 'Ulster-Scots and Irish unionist resource',
summed up the narrative in 2003:

> There are, it's suspected, some Bogside homes that still have a souvenir
> of Apprentice Boys of Derry history sitting on their mantlepieces [sic].
> Because, on the night when the IRA blew up Walker's Monument, people

from the republican stronghold, which lay in its shadow, scrambled for shattered pieces of the magnificent structure that had been treated with great reverence by the loyal order.[20]

Day asserts further that only one leg was recovered from the original statue. This strand of narrative echoes the initial report of the *Derry Journal*, which indicated that 'when it became evident that the pillar had been felled, hundreds of people took to the streets to collect pieces of debris as souvenirs'.[21]

However, the *Irish Independent* report of the bombing notes the remarkable degree to which the explosion appeared to have been controlled. Very little debris fell into the Bogside after the blast as most of the rubble came straight down and remained around the base of the pillar and within the city walls. The paper asserts, and the Apprentice Boys maintain today, that 'the only damage to the statue is on the right forearm, which has been broken off. The hand has been recovered'.[22] In fact, the debris came down so cleanly that the *Independent* also immediately postulated another scenario, which survives still in the myth-narratives of the bombing today – that the bombers who brought down Nelson's pillar in Dublin in 1966 assisted in the explosion in Derry. The report noted not only that the blast was 'reminiscent of the downfall of Nelson in Dublin seven years ago', but also that the Walker memorial 'was blown up by expert bombers who appeared to have used the same techniques which brought down Nelson', for, like Walker, the latter's initial destruction caused very little damage to surrounding buildings and structures. Famously, in that case, the army's secondary controlled explosion to remove the remnants of the monument caused much more significant destruction to the surrounding area.[23] In any case, the identity of the Derry bombers has never been revealed and the link to Dublin is unsubstantiated.

If pieces of debris were collected by local residents, they are likely to have been chunks of exploded pillar, which were indeed plentiful. The claim occasionally repeated in some nationalist quarters that a young Catholic boy found the head of the statue among the gravestones in the churchyard of St Augustine's and subsequently ransomed it back to the Apprentice Boys is surely apocryphal. The head rests today in the newly built Siege Museum as it was too damaged to be repaired when the organization restored the statue in the early 1990s, and even in its decapitated form, its larger-than-life, solid stone mass requires several adult men to lift. Nevertheless, these narratives, and the apparent interest of each community in appropriating some piece of the bombing mythology for themselves, demonstrate the continued importance of the Walker monument in the symbolic, if not the physical, landscape. Claims of possession such as those in these narratives enhance the position of each side in the symbolic expansionary contest that developed within the framework of actual political struggle.

THE MEMORIAL TODAY

The most significant element of the Walker Testimonial in its heyday had been the statue of the governor himself, and in the absence of the full complement of commemorative accoutrements in the wake of the 1973 bombing, the statue came to develop an even greater significance in the minds of the Apprentice Boys. They have continued to use the figure as a symbol of defence of loyalism even after the formal end of the Troubles to enhance the standing of their organization and to attract visitors to their hall and museum. The last few decades have proven them very successful in these efforts, but not without consequences. This final section examines the fortunes of the Apprentice Boys and their monument after the end of official hostilities and in the era of shared community-building in Derry.

The 81-foot pillar on which Walker perched for 145 years has never been repaired. As the pillar had been destroyed during the course of the Troubles, the Apprentice Boys qualified to appeal to the Northern Ireland Office for compensation for its loss. In the spring of 1989, the organization received £800,000 on the condition that the monument would not be rebuilt.[24] The funds were used instead to restore the statue of Walker, and in 1992 it was rededicated in a small garden adjoining the Apprentice Boys' Memorial Hall on Society Street. The statue's head, left arm and other damaged elements were replaced, and each piece joined to the original torso in such a way as to preserve as much of the 19th-century statue as possible. The two annual siege commemorations continued to be held, and the empty plinth that formerly held Walker's pillar and statue – itself also restored in 1992 with the compensatory funds – remain a symbolic stopping point for the Apprentice Boys along their annual commemorative parade route in both August and December. Although an effigy of Lundy was never burned again at the site of the Walker Testimonial, the Apprentice Boys continued to set them alight in a number of alternative locations until the restorations were complete in 1992, when the site at Bishop's Gate was chosen for the purpose. It remains today the new customary location for the conflagration.[25]

It is worth noting here that unlike the commemorative impulse of the 19th century, in which actual objects connected with a historical event were not necessarily venerated – recall the discussion in the first chapter of the replacement and 'enhancement' of the medieval city gate – the original plinth and statue continue to hold importance for the modern Apprentice Boys. Through these restorations, they have attempted to regain some of the lost power of their destroyed monument by maintaining its most significant feature, the sculpture itself, and by continuing to incorporate the plinth, which they decorate with orange banners and from which they still fly the customary crimson flag, into the modified new rituals of commemoration that they have been forced to

6. Apprentice Boys memorial garden on Society Street, 2006.

adopt by the loss of their traditional symbols. The Walker monument has thus been kept alive in symbolic ritual and practice, despite its physical destruction.

In late July of 2010, however, the reconstituted Walker statue again came under attack. Vandals, whose identities have never been ascertained but who are believed to have been republican activists, repeatedly struck the statue with something very like a sledgehammer. The assailants smashed off the figure's left arm and caused significant damage to its face as well as other areas.[26] In light of the Good Friday Agreement and the end of the physical violence to which the city's earlier symbolic conflict had been bound, this new attack was universally seen as reprehensible. Pat Ramsay, former mayor of Derry and nationalist SDLP representative to the Northern Ireland assembly, asserted of the attack that 'the people of Derry will be appalled to learn of this act of wanton vandalism. Respect for different cultures and traditions is essential as we strive to build a shared society and promote Derry as a shared city.' Emphasizing that all forms of the conflict must end, and alluding to the recent announcement of Derry as the winner of the inaugural UK City of Culture designation, Ramsay continued, 'Derry has been in the media spotlight for so many good reasons lately. We will not let anyone drag us back into the past.'[27]

Nevertheless, within some quarters of the city, the Walker statue continues to be seen as representative of loyalist symbolism, its power never completely having faded. Indeed, still today the empty plinth can often be seen covered in paint bombs and political graffiti applied from below the walls. For this reason, the Apprentice Boys organization, although they still continued to hope that eventually the Testimonial will be rebuilt, resolved to keep the statue inside their Memorial Hall where it could be kept safe from attack. They repaired it once more, and although it required a second round of new appendages, they endeavoured once again to keep as much of the original statue and its 1992 additions intact as possible. In March 2013, the statue was placed inside the entryway of the Memorial Hall, which housed the Apprentice Boys' Siege Heroes Museum, a space dedicated to the history of the group and the siege of Derry as they remember it. In interviews conducted at that time, members of the organization emphasized the importance of the original elements, and, as suggested at the outset of this chapter, the statue's continued existence and its harlequin composition lent credence to the claims for its longevity and indestructibility in spite of persistent attack. In a moment when the symbols of loyalist devotion to the siege were under attack, and the organization saw itself very much on the defensive, this strategy of activating the discourse of survival and utilizing objectified capital in the form of the original pieces of the Walker statue served as a kind of bulwark against detractors. But as the situation changed, the group's strategies for appeal to and application of that symbolic capital changed as well.

At the end of 2012, the Apprentice Boys received a grant of £2.2m from the European Union's Peace III Programme, governed by the Special EU Programmes Body. The grant was intended to finance a refurbishment of the Memorial Hall and the building of a new interpretative visitor's centre and museum on the site of the adjoining memorial garden that had formerly held Walker's statue, and which at the time stood closed and empty.[28] The new 5,000 square foot facility, renamed simply 'The Siege Museum', opened officially in October 2015 and its founders declared their intention to 'welcome individuals and groups from all communities to the Siege Museum, where they can view and understand the rich history of the Maiden City'.[29] The centrepiece of the new space is the Walker statue, but its situation is now much altered. It has been plastered over completely, leaving a shining white uniformity to its whole body, and stands atop a custom pedestal on the second floor of the museum in front of a large plate-glass window overlooking the street below.

Both the position and the appearance of the statue bear examination in the context of symbolic contest and Derry's iconographic landscape. In its previous location in the entryway of the old museum space at the front of the Memorial Hall, the statue stood at ground level. Its pointing left arm gestured in the direction of the inner doorway and thus welcomed visitors into the museum. The 'Frankenstein's monster' effect of its appearance suggested perseverance and enduring tradition in the face of opposition, and the combined effect was one of an embattled figure inviting communion with and sympathy for its history

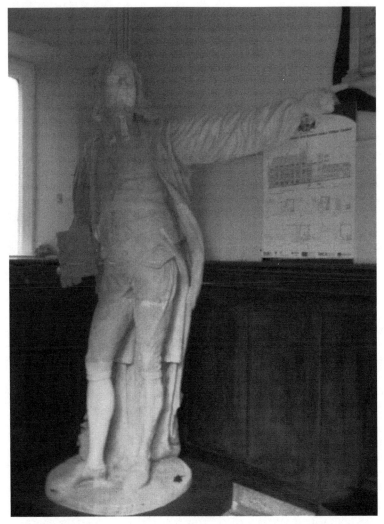

7. Reconstituted statue of Walker inside Apprentice Boys' Memorial Hall, 2013.

and traditions. This undoubtedly reflected the position of the Apprentice Boys within the community of Derry at the time. With the acquisition of EU Peace funding and a new position of civic importance for its visitors' centre, however, this sense of embattlement seems to have disappeared, to be replaced with one of pride and perhaps even resurgent triumphalism. The statue's new position reflects quite literally an increase in standing. It rests much higher off the ground on a new pedestal, and stands in front of a large, second-storey window where it is clearly visible from the ground below. Whereas, in its former location, its left arm pointed inward to the museum, the statue now has been intentionally positioned such that it replicates the original pose and direction of the statue on top of the Testimonial pillar – pointing its left arm provocatively toward the Foyle where the English ships arrived to relieve the siege. In this arrangement, the statue can be seen gesturing to its original purpose even when the museum is closed, and it remains safe from attack inside its well-secured display space.

Now that the Apprentice Boys are no longer in a defensive stance, and the statue stands little chance of further vandalism, it is tempting to see a reflection of this attitude in the new physical appearance of the statue as well. Gone are its seams and joins, which had shown so clearly the incorporation of the new within the old. Gone are the visible remnants of the original statue with its weathered stone and its new additions of slightly lighter hue. Instead, the whole of the figure has been covered over with a bright white coating, suggesting at once both an unassailable historical (and literal) integrity and the abandonment of a sense of value in the original elements. The new appearance belies the history of the statue – a history full of conflict and struggle – to suggest a permanence and invincibility that has grounding only in the mythological narrative of the siege commemorations. The history of the statue's legacy of symbolic conflict, once visible in its very seams, has been erased entirely in its new iteration. One hopes it may ultimately benefit the cause of shared community-building to plaster over the visible signs of conflict in the city's history and thus present a picture of unity. However, underlying divisions over the symbolic iconography of Derry still remain and they parallel those cracks which are still present in the Walker statue despite no longer being apparent on the surface. It remains to be seen whether these divisions, if left intact at their core, will remain hidden where they lie.

Examining the destruction of the Walker Testimonial, as well as its associated enduring myth-narratives, demonstrates that the decades of aggregate symbolic capital it had embodied culminated in its identification as a target in the symbolic conflict embedded within the political and physical struggle of the Troubles. While Simon Harrison's model for categorizing the types of such conflict can be usefully employed in understanding the functions of the opposing communities' interactions with the monument, it nevertheless fails to explain the dimensions of symbolism that the Walker statue and its plinth maintained through the successive phases of commemoration, narrativization and reconstruction and display. This cycle of destruction and restoration over more than four decades suggests that the relevance of the monument has not yet diminished in the symbolic landscape of Derry, and that the statue retains enough currency and embodied capital within the loyalist community (and in the eyes of some republicans) to make it first vulnerable to attack and then a literal picture of invincibility. The Apprentice Boys have altered their discourse surrounding the statue as their own position has shifted in Derry society. With the acquisition of financing and a new sense of civic positioning, the organization has altered

8. Newly restored Walker statue at EU-funded Siege Museum, 2016.

its utilization of the symbolic capital objectified in the statue in a manner that reflects its position. Our understanding of the ways in which such capital can be marshalled for contests over symbolism bears much relevance for the success of peace and reconciliation efforts in divided communities.

Conclusion

The violent and illustrative history of the Walker Testimonial of the Apprentice Boys of Derry has much to reveal about the patterns of symbolic conflict in the city and the processes through which symbolic capital transactions occur. The longstanding existence of commemorations of the siege of Derry in various forms throughout the late 18th and 19th centuries provides the backdrop for understanding the role that the Walker memorial occupied in the city from its creation in 1826–8, through to its destruction in 1973, and down to the restorations and displays of recent years. Almost as soon as the monument was dedicated, it began to accumulate symbolic capital through a series of transactional processes enacted by members of both the Catholic and Protestant communities. The Apprentice Boys fuelled the process through the relocation of significant elements of the siege celebrations to the monument and its establishment as the preferred location for the burning of the Lundy effigy every December. As the political climate in the city shifted in the late 19th century, so too did the meaning and symbolic importance of the Walker memorial, and as the violent, physical conflict of the Troubles emerged in the third quarter of the 20th century, the monument too became the most obvious target in the accompanying symbolic conflict. The focus of this book on the processes that enabled these transformations and interactions to occur provides a window into the means through which divided communities carry out symbolic conflict.

The mythological narrativization strategies employed by both the monument's supporters and detractors are equally significant for our understanding of these processes. Narrative strategies of transferring symbolic capital can be just as effective as ritual commemorative practices when the setting allows. Stories of the statue's original 'lost' sword, likely concocted by Thomas D'Arcy McGee in the mid-19th century and still thriving today, served to suggest the eventual triumph of nationalism and to diminish the standing of the monument along the sliding scale of relative symbolic value. Propaganda tales and anecdotal assertions of local residents carrying off pieces of the monument's exploded rubble further suggest the mythological power of the object while simultaneously creating conditions in which it would continue to accrue or lose objectified symbolic capital. That such stories continue to circulate in contemporary Derry and indeed in scholarship about the city reveals the extent of the impact it has made in the symbolic landscape.

This short book has attempted to explain the development of the symbolism attached to the Walker Testimonial and to rectify the absence of a full historical investigation into its lifecycle and position. It presents in so doing not only a history of the monument, but an examination of symbolic conflict in the city of Derry. I have offered suggestions for understanding how a divisive monument can come to be so symbolically powerful within a contested setting, and the ways in which it maintains that power and resonance in that setting even after its destruction. Derry city in many ways continues to find itself enveloped in symbolic contestation, and the recent opening of the newest Apprentice Boys museum indicates that their symbols and traditions – and especially the statue of Walker – will continue to remain a part of this narrative. It is hoped that the arguments proposed and the insights afforded here will lay the groundwork for future investigations of the symbolic conflict in Derry itself, as well as those represented by the destruction and vandalism of sites of memory across the Irish landscape in the 19th and 20th centuries, for it is certainly a rich and valuable field that remains understudied in the professional historical academy. Studies of this nature have much to reveal about the processes of conflict, and thereby hold the potential to make important contributions to endeavours to build lasting peace and shared communities.

Notes

INTRODUCTION

1 The very name of the city is itself a battleground of symbolic conflict. I here follow a trend in scholarly writing, that employs 'Derry' when referring to the city itself and 'Londonderry' in reference to the surrounding county. All subsequent usage will follow this format.

2 Bloody Sunday has itself become the subject of much popular commemoration and scholarly interest. Of recent particular interest are: Graham Dawson, 'Trauma, place and the politics of memory: Bloody Sunday, Derry, 1972–2004', *History Workshop Journal*, 59 (2005), 151–78; and Jack Santino, 'Between commemoration and social activism: spontaneous shrines, grassroots memorialization and the public ritualesque in Derry' in Peter Jan Margry and Cristina Sánchez-Carretero (eds), *Grassroots memorials: the politics of memorializing traumatic death* (New York, 2011), pp 97–107. On memory and the Troubles more broadly, see Jim Smyth (ed.), *Remembering the Troubles: contesting the recent past in Northern Ireland* (Notre Dame, IN, 2017).

3 The literature on siege mythology and commemorations has steadily expanded since the 1990s. See especially Ian McBride, *The siege of Derry in Ulster Protestant mythology* (Dublin, 1997); William Kelly (ed.), *The sieges of Derry* (Dublin, 2001); T.G. Fraser, 'The siege: its history and legacy, 1688–1889' in Gerard O'Brien (ed.), *Derry & Londonderry: history & society* (Dublin, 1999), pp 379–403; James Kelly, '"The Glorious and Immortal Memory": commemoration and Protestant identity in Ireland 1660–1800', *Proceedings of the Royal Irish Academy*, 94C (1990), 25–52; Neil Maddox, 'Commemorating the siege: the Williamite marching tradition in nineteenth-century Derry', *History Studies*, 6 (2005), available from: https://ssrn.com/abstract=1532928; and most recently, James White McAuley, 'Memory, narratives, and popular culture' and 'Paramilitarism and commemoration' in James White McAuley (ed.), *Very British rebels? the culture and politics of Ulster loyalism* (London, 2016) pp 95–138. On the siege itself, see chapter one.

4 McBride, *The siege of Derry*, pp 13–14.

5 Pierre Bourdieu, 'The forms of capital', originally published as 'Ökonomisches Kapital, kulturelles Kapital, soziales Kapital' in Reinhard Kreckel (ed.), *Soziale Ungleichheiten*, Soziale Welt, Sonderheft 2, (Goettingen, 1983), pp 183–98.

6 Pierre Bourdieu, *The logic of practice* (Cambridge, 1990), pp 112–21.

7 Simon Harrison, 'Four types of symbolic conflict', *Journal of the Royal Anthropological Institute*, 1:2 (1995), 255–72.

8 Elisabetta Viggiani, *Talking stones: the politics of memorialization in post-conflict Northern Ireland* (New York, 2014), pp 150–72, especially pp 154–5.

9 On the significance of Derry's geography, demography and the location of the monument, see chapter one. The 'Bogside' is a predominantly Catholic area of the city located outside the old city walls. At the time of the 1973 bombing, Catholic houses in the neighbourhood still backed up against the walls directly underneath the Walker Testimonial.

1. EARLY SIEGE CELEBRATIONS AND THE CONSTRUCTION OF THE MEMORIAL

1 The Parades Commission for Northern Ireland, PAR/72215, ABOD Associated

Clubs, Londonderry, 13 Aug. 2016,
available from: http://www.
paradescommission.org/viewparade.
aspx?id=59768, accessed 24 May 2017.

2 *Belfast News Letter*, 'Apprentice Boys
Parade to Climax Maiden City
Festival', 10 Aug. 2016; *Belfast Telegraph*,
'In pictures: crowds enjoy annual
Apprentice Boys Relief of Derry parade',
14 Aug. 2016.

3 Connla Young, *Irish News*, 'Thousands
attend annual Derry Apprentice Boys
parade', 15 Aug. 2016.

4 The author of the conspiracy published
his claims at his own expense: Titus
Oates, *A true narrative of the horrid plot and
conspiracy of the popish party against the life
of his sacred majesty, the government, and the
Protestant religion* (London, 1679). John
Pollock's analysis remains the classic
account of the conspiracy: *The popish
plot: a study in the history of the reign of
Charles II* (Cambridge, 1944). On the
effect of the 'plot' in Ireland and its role
in stoking fears of a Catholic rebellion
against the Protestant ruling class, see
John Gibney, *Ireland and the popish plot*
(London, 2009).

5 A recent account of the revolution
argues that James II's interest in repealing
the laws governing religious non-
conformity led to the development
by his opponents of a carefully crafted
sense of grievance about the abrogation
of Protestant freedoms and a strong
narrative of victimization that would
underpin a movement to depose him.
Scott Sowerby, *Making toleration: the
repealers and the Glorious Revolution*
(Cambridge, MA, 2013). See also Robert
Beddard (ed.), *The revolutions of 1688*
(Oxford, 1981).

6 On Tyrconnell's career, see Carlo Gébler,
The siege of Derry: a history (London,
2005), pp 37–50. Tyrconnell would
be the last lord deputy as the position
became known as that of lord lieutenant
after 1690.

7 General accounts of the conflict include
Richard Doherty, *The Williamite War in
Ireland* (Dublin, 1998), and John Childs,
The Williamite Wars in Ireland, 1688–1691
(London, 2008).

8 Jonathan Bardon's monumental survey
of the Plantation remains the most
accessible, if not the most balanced: *The
Plantation of Ulster: the British colonization
of the North of Ireland in the seventeenth
century* (London, 2012).

9 The British empire adopted the
Gregorian calendar in 1752, which is
11 days ahead of the old Julian calendar
in use until that point. The Apprentice
Boys today use the Gregorian calendar
to mark the dates of the siege events,
placing the Shutting of the Gates on 18
December and the Relief of the Siege
on 12 August. I follow the original
Julian dates in this account of the siege
itself, and adopt the Gregorian dates at
the moment in the narrative where the
historical shift occurred.

10 The historiography of the siege is
considerable. Its bicentenary alone
occasioned the production of a number
of good general accounts: Brian Lacy,
The siege of Derry (Norwich, 1989) and
Patrick Macrory, *The siege of Derry*
(Oxford, 1988). Partisan treatments
appeared as well, including that of the
future first minister of Northern Ireland,
Peter Robinson, published while its
author resided in Cell 18, D Wing, in
Belfast's Crumlin Road Prison: *Their
cry was 'no surrender'* (Belfast, 1988). See
also the magisterial Cecil Davis Milligan,
History of the siege of Londonderry 1689
(Belfast, 1951); Tony Gray, *No surrender!
The siege of Londonderry 1689* (London,
1975); Carlo Gébler, *The siege of Derry: a
history* (London, 2005); John Hempton
(ed.), *The siege and history of Londonderry*
(Londonderry, 1861). The most famous
contemporary accounts come from
Governor Walker himself, *A true account
of the siege of London-Derry*, edited by
Revd Philip Dwyer and appearing as
The siege of Londonderry in 1689 (London,
1893), and the rival account of John
Mackenzie, *Mackenzie's narrative of
the siege*, reproduced in Hempton,
Siege and history; also of interest is the
contemporary journal of Thomas Ash,
later printed by his granddaughter:
*A circumstantial account of the siege of
Londonderry from a MS written on the spot*

and at the time (Londonderry, 1792). On
the terminology of the 'Apprentice Boys'
and the 'Closing of the Gates', see T.G.
Fraser, 'The siege: its history and legacy,
1688–1889' in O'Brien (ed.), Derry and
Londonderry, pp 379–404, at 380.

11 Walker, A true account, pp 17–18. It
is worth noting the parallel with the
later escape from Scotland by means of
disguise conducted by the Jacobite prince
Charles Edward Stuart – Bonnie Prince
Charlie – who led the last major Jacobite
uprising of 1745 in the final attempt
to restore the line of succession of his
grandfather James II.

12 Apprentice Boys of Derry General
Committee, 'Relief of Londonderry',
website of the Associated Clubs of the
Apprentice Boys of Derry, http://www.
apprenticeboysofderry.org/relief-of-
londonderry, accessed 30 May 2017.

13 Walker, True account, p. 30.

14 McBride, The siege of Derry, pp 32–7.

15 Ash, Circumstantial account, pp 101–3.

16 Cecil Davis Milligan, The Walker Club
centenary: a history of the Apprentice Boys
of Derry and biographical notes on Governor
Walker (Londonderry, 1944), p. 9.

17 McBride, The siege of Derry, p. 35.
The account appears in R.M. Sibbett,
Orangeism in Ireland and throughout the
empire, 2 vols (2nd ed., London, 1939), pp
190–1. For the less convincing argument
in favour of accepting this source, see
Milligan, The Walker Club, pp 10–11.

18 Bishop Nicolson's diaries: part V, bishop
of Barrow-on-Furness, p. 19, quoted in
Milligan, The Walker Club, p. 12. See also
Hempton, Siege and history, p. 411 and
McBride, The siege of Derry, p. 36.

19 The study of early modern memory and
commemoration is quickly developing
a vast literature, but in the English
and British contexts, valuable studies
include: David Cressy, Bonfires and
bells: national memory and the Protestant
calendar in Elizabethan and Stuart England
(Los Angeles, 1989); David Cressy,
'The Fifth of November remembered'
in Roy Porter (ed.), Myths of the
English (Cambridge, 1992), pp 75–79;
Ian W. Archer, 'The arts and acts of
memorialization in early modern
London' in J.F. Merritt (ed.), Imagining

early modern London (Cambridge, 2001);
Peter Sherlock, Monuments and memory in
early modern England (Aldershot, 2008).

20 Londonderry Journal, 5 Aug. 1772. The
anniversary of the relief arrived just
a few months after the first issue of
the new periodical went to press. See
Hempton, Siege and history, pp 415–16.

21 Londonderry Journal, 14 Nov. 1775.
Quoted in Hempton, Siege and history, p.
419. See also Milligan, The Walker Club,
p. 17.

22 McBride, The siege of Derry, p. 33.

23 Hempton, Siege and history, p. 421;
McBride, The siege of Derry, p. 38.

24 J. Stewart, Baronscourt, to earl of
Abercorn, 29 Aug. 1780, Public Record
Office of Northern Ireland, T2541/
IA1/13/47, hereafter PRONI, also
quoted in McBride, The siege of Derry,
p. 39, following Peter Smyth, '"Our
Cloud-Cap't Grenadiers": the Volunteers
as a military force', Irish Sword, 13
(1978–9), 204.

25 Participating military companies through
the end of the century included: the
Londonderry Artillery (1783), the 13th
Regiment (1786), the 16th Regiment
(1787), the 46th Regiment (1788),
the 28th Regiment (1789), the 48th
Regiment (1790), the Fifeshire Fencibles
(1795), the Tipperary Militia and the
Londonderry Cavalry (1796), the
garrison infantry and cavalry (1797) and
the Tipperary Militia again (1798). See
Hempton, Siege and history, pp 422–5.

26 George Douglas, The Poliorciad, or poems
of the siege (Londonderry, 1789), reprinted
in idem, Derriana – a collection of papers
relative to the siege of Derry, and illustrative
of the revolution of 1688 (Londonderry,
1794); Milligan, The Walker Club, p. 20;
McBride, The siege of Derry, p. 40. For
more on the burning of Lundy effigies,
see the discussion in the second chapter.

27 Thomas Colby, Ordnance Survey memoir
for the Derry parish of Templemore (Dublin,
1837), reprinted with introduction by
Tony Crowe (Limavady, 1990), p. 49. See
also Fraser, 'The siege', pp 389–90.

28 Colby, Ordnance Survey memoir, p. 70.

29 Milligan, The Walker Club, pp 19–20.

30 Fraser, 'The siege', p. 390. On the
decision to erect the monument, see John

Graham, *A history of the siege of Derry and defence of Enniskillen in 1688 and 1689* (2nd ed., Dublin, 1829), p. 282.

31 On the effects of this changing climate, see Jim Smyth (ed.), *Revolution, counter-revolution and union: Ireland in the 1790s* (Cambridge, 2000), especially the editor's introduction tracing the historiographical debate.

32 McBride, *The siege of Derry*, p. 42.

33 Ibid.

34 On lower-class Irish radicalism during the age of the French Revolution, and especially civil protest, see Jim Smyth, *The men of no property* (London, 1998); see also Fraser, 'The siege', pp 390–1.

35 Hempton, *Siege and history*, pp 440–45; McBride, *The siege of Derry*, p. 47.

36 *Londonderry Journal*, 28 Oct. 1811.

37 Indeed, Milligan notes unquestioningly the implausible assertion of the 'Old Derryman' that 'as far back as he had been able to trace the recollection of the oldest residents, it had been the custom of the inhabitants, of all descriptions, to celebrate, as festivals, the days of the commencement and the raising of the Siege in various ways; and, among others, by embellishing their houses and persons with orange lilies or ribbons'. Milligan, *The Walker Club*, 13.

38 McBride, *The siege of Derry*, p. 47.

39 Hempton, *Siege and history*, p. 441; Milligan, *The Walker Club*, 21.

40 Hempton, *Siege and history*, p. 445. See also Fraser, 'The siege', p. 392.

41 Milligan, *The Walker Club*, 22; Hempton, *Siege and history*, p. 446.

42 Colby, *Ordnance Survey memoir*, pp 197–8.

43 Milligan, *The Walker Club*, p. 22; Hempton, *Siege and history*, p. 446.

44 Milligan, *The Walker Club*, p. 71.

45 McBride, *The siege of Derry*, p. 51.

46 Billy Moore, secretary general of the Associated Clubs of the Apprentice Boys of Derry, interview with author, 31 July 2013.

47 The pillar was built separately by a group identified in Simpson's *Annals* only as Henry, Mullins and McMahon. The total cost of the project is recorded at £4,200. Robert Simpson, *The annals of Derry, showing the rise and progress of the town from the earliest accounts on record to the*

plantation under King James I – 1613. *And thence of the city of Londonderry to the present time* (Londonderry, 1847), p. 247. For the suggestion that the statue originally held a sword in its left hand, see the discussion in the second chapter in this volume.

48 Milligan, *The Walker Club*, p. 72.

49 Brian Lacy, *Siege city: the story of Derry and Londonderry* (Belfast, 1990), p. 169.

50 Moore, interview with author, 31 July 2013.

51 Quoted in McBride, *The siege of Derry*, p. 51, excerpted from James Gregg, *The Apprentice Boys of Derry* and *No Surrender! or, Protestant heroism triumphant over Popish malignity; being a succinct and interesting account of the siege of Derry* (London, 1827), p. 3. The title of Gregg's work ought to remove any remaining ambiguity regarding his position on the sectarian nature of the siege narrative.

52 Colby, *Ordnance Survey memoir*, pp 119–20.

2. THE MYTHOLOGIZING AND UTILIZATION OF THE WALKER TESTIMONIAL, 1826–70

1 Party Processus (Ireland) Act, 2 and 3 William IV, c. 113.

2 Neil P. Maddox, '"A melancholy record": the story of the nineteenth-century Irish Party Processions Acts', *Irish Jurist*, 39 (2004), 243.

3 Ibid., 247.

4 Ibid., 248.

5 Colby, *Ordnance Survey memoir*, p. 119. See also Fraser, 'The siege', p. 392.

6 'Opening of the gates of London-Derry', *Chutes Western Herald*, 18 Aug. 1832.

7 Douglas, *Poliarciad*, p. 65.

8 David Cressy, 'The Fifth of November remembered' in Roy Porter (ed.), *Myths of the English* (Cambridge, 1992), pp 75–9; William L. Sachse, 'The mob and revolution of 1688', *Journal of British Studies*, 4 (1964), 23–40.

9 McBride, *The siege of Derry*, p. 41.

10 In 2009, the *Sentinel* cited the 1832 burning of Lundy as the first, and it is certainly possible that the practice did not occur between 1788 and that year, but on balance, the available evidence

tends toward the establishment of something like a new tradition by the early 1830s.

11 The date may well be a bit later than 1832, but the painting confirms the existence of this symbolic ritual in the early 1830s in a context independent of the Walker Testimonial. The pillar's status in relation to the burning of Lundy remained secondary.

12 *Londonderry Sentinel*, 22 Dec. 1832.

13 Hempton, *Siege and history*, p. 449; Milligan, *The Walker Club*, p. 23; McBride, *The siege of Derry*, p. 52.

14 Act 13 and 14 Victoria, c. 2.

15 On the culture of sectarian violence at this time, see Sean Farrell, 'Urbanization and sectarian rioting in mid-Victorian Ulster' in Sean Farrell, *Rituals and riots: sectarian violence and political culture in Ulster, 1784–1886* (Lexington, KY, 2000), pp. 125–53. For the contested incident at Dolly's Brae, see Richard McMahon, *Homicide in pre-Famine and Famine Ireland* (Liverpool, 2013), p. 131.

16 Act 23 and 24, Victoria, c. 141.

17 Hempton, *Siege and history*, p. 453; Milligan, *The Walker Club*, p. 43.

18 *Irish Times*, 19 Dec. 1860.

19 Ibid.

20 Hempton, *Siege and history*, p. 458.

21 Fraser, 'The siege', p. 395. See also Aiken McClelland, *William Johnstone of Ballykilbeg* (Lurgan, 1990), chapter 4.

22 McBride, *The siege of Derry*, p. 52.

23 Fraser, 'The siege', p. 396.

24 *Report of commissioners of inquiry, 1869, into the riots and disturbances in the city of Londonderry* (Dublin, 1869).

25 Ibid.

26 Ibid.

27 Milligan, *The Walker Club*, p. 44.

28 Ibid.

29 Fraser, 'The siege', pp 397–8.

30 Milligan, *The Walker Club*, p. 45.

31 Ibid.

32 *Derry Journal*, 17 Dec. 1870. The incident appears also in the *Londonderry Sentinel*, 20 Dec. 1870.

33 Milligan, *The Walker Club*, pp 46–7.

34 McBride, *The siege of Derry*, p. 51, following Richard Hayward, *In praise of Ulster* (Belfast, 1938), p. 260. The story

also appears in a retrospective piece in the *Derry Journal*, 'Siege hero Walker felled in midnight blast', 23 July 2010, which has been cited even by a blogger for the National Library of Ireland in a description of a photograph of the Walker statue from the Lawrence Photo Collection held at the library: NLI, L_CAB_00592.

35 Thomas Babington Macaulay, *The history of England from the succession of James the Second*, 5 vols (London, 1848–61), i, p. 257.

36 Fraser, 'The siege', p. 393.

37 John Graham, *The history of the siege of Londonderry and defence of Enniskillen in 1688 and 1689* (2nd ed., Dublin, 1829). See also Milligan, *The Walker Club*, p. 71 for a discussion of this frontispiece.

38 Graham, *History of the siege*, p. 228.

39 Thomas Mellon, *Thomas Mellon and his times* (Pittsburgh, PA, 1994), p. 313. Mellon's autobiography was originally written in 1885 for the benefit of his family alone and was unpublished until this printing. The erroneous description of the monument was repeated by his recent biographer, James Mellon, who corrects the name of Walker, but not the story of the sword. See James Mellon, *The judge: a life of Thomas Mellon, founder of a fortune* (New Haven, CT, 2011), pp 324–5.

40 Thomas Mellon, *Thomas Mellon and his times*, p. 314.

41 Walker had been scheduled to be named bishop of Derry, but died at the Boyne before he could be appointed.

42 Thomas D'Arcy McGee, *A popular history of Ireland: from the earliest period to the emancipation of the Catholics, volume II* (Glasgow, 1869), pp 803–4. For more on McGee and emancipation, see David A. Wilson, *Thomas D'Arcy McGee: the extreme moderate, 1857–1868* (Montreal, 2011), especially p. 193.

3. THE MONUMENT DURING THE TROUBLES

1 For a description of this event, see Philip Orr, *The road to the Somme: men of the Ulster Division tell their story* (Belfast, 1967), p. 116.

2 For an in-depth, although often problematic, assessment of the period, see